D1567976

This book was published
with the generous support of

Furthermore

a program of the J. M. Kaplan Fund.

Designing the Good Life

Florida A&M University, Tallahassee

Florida Atlantic University, Boca Raton

Florida Gulf Coast University, Ft. Myers

Florida International University, Miami

Florida State University, Tallahassee

University of Central Florida, Orlando

University of Florida, Gainesville

University of North Florida, Jacksonville

University of South Florida, Tampa

University of West Florida, Pensacola

Designing the Good Life

NORMAN M. GILLER AND THE DEVELOPMENT OF MIAMI MODERNISM

Norman M. Giller and Sarah Giller Nelson

UNIVERSITY PRESS OF FLORIDA   Gainesville · Tallahassee · Tampa · Boca Raton · Pensacola · Orlando · Miami · Jacksonville · Ft. Myers

Copyright 2007 by Norman M. Giller and Sarah Giller Nelson
Printed in China on acid-free paper

12   11   10   09   08   07   6   5   4   3   2   1

Library of Congress Cataloging-in-Publication Data
Giller, Norman M.
Designing the good life : Norman M. Giller and the development
of Miami modernism / Norman M. Giller and Sarah Giller Nelson.
    p. cm.
Includes bibliographical references and index.
ISBN 978-0-8130-3071-5 (alk. paper)
1. Giller, Norman M.—Themes, motives. 2. Architecture—Florida—
Miami—20th century. 3. Miami (Fla.)—Buildings, structures, etc.
I. Nelson, Sarah Giller. II. Title.
NA737.G534A4 2007
720.92—dc22   2007002821

The University Press of Florida is the scholarly publishing agency
for the State University System of Florida, comprising Florida A&M
University, Florida Atlantic University, Florida Gulf Coast University,
Florida International University, Florida State University, University
of Central Florida, University of Florida, University of North Florida,
University of South Florida, and University of West Florida.

University Press of Florida
15 Northwest 15th Street
Gainesville, FL 32611-2079
www.upf.com

Front matter photographs: *page i*, Diplomat Hotel, Hollywood, Florida,
1957–58 (demolished), hyperbolic paraboloid entrance; *page ii*, Carillon
Hotel, Miami Beach, 1957–58 (altered), rendering; *right*, Thunderbird
Motel, Sunny Isles, 1955, lobby.

Contents

Foreword

Norman M. Giller is one of the most prolific exponents of postwar regional Modernism that has come to be known as Miami Modern, or MiMo, which can be defined as the architecture characteristic of a particular time—the prosperity and sunny optimism of postwar America—and a particular place—subtropical Florida.

Giller's own career bridges Art Deco from his early years working as a draftsman in the office of Henry Hohauser, the architect who is credited with making Miami modern. In its prime, from the housing and tourist boom after World War II until the air-conditioned excesses of the early 1970s, MiMo, like Art Deco before it, was not a term used by practicing architects. Giller is quick to point out that architects of the time would simply have said they were designing Modern or contemporary buildings.

Nonetheless, MiMo circumscribes a coherent architecture. In addition to Giller, major architects whose work falls under this capacious umbrella of subtropical Modernism include Morris Lapidus, Melvin Grossman, and Gilbert M. Fein, all based in Miami. Alternative approaches to subtropical Modernism can be seen in the works of Alfred Browning Parker, Kenneth Treister, and Igor B. Polevitzky.

Giller's work is distinguished by a zestful use of applied symbolism to rigorous Modernist construction. As he notes in his introduction to this volume, the automobile had a tremendous influence on every aspect of South Florida living. Giller's designs are packed with curb appeal, from his eye-grabbing themed motels like the Thunderbird Motel (Sunny Isles, 1955) to the abstract "accordion wall" of the original Carillon Hotel (Miami Beach, 1957–58), which resembled an oversized automobile grille cast in concrete. His multiwinged Driftwood Motel (Sunny Isles, 1951–53; demolished) was spatially sequenced to be appreciated from the vantage point of a moving automobile.

Like much of populist postwar Modernism, as characterized by the Populuxe and Googie styles, Giller's designs incorporated the vocabulary of contemporary Hollywood cinema: widescreen horizontal compositions like the Driftwood, lush application of color like the imported green tile for the pylon of the Giller Building (Miami Beach, 1955–61) in contrast to the chasteness of the International Style, and even a sequentialization and framing of space perhaps subconsciously influenced by sweeping Cinemascope camera moves.

Giller's designs can also be viewed within the broader context of a turn to organic and biomorphic forms in the postwar period in contrast to the largely streamlined design of the Depression era. His use of fluid forms began with the Copa City Night Club (Miami Beach, 1948; altered) with the *parti* of a grand piano and an extraordinary curving, columnless interior by Norman Bel Geddes, a streamline force majeure whose career spanned the postwar period.

**Ocean Palm Motel,
Sunny Isles, 1949.
Sign. Photograph,
2001.**

Designing the Good Life is a fascinating look at how an individual architect's style evolves within a wider cultural framework. As a school, MiMo is significantly indebted to Frank Lloyd Wright, from the flat roofs, cantilevers, and planarity of his Prairie style to the circular compositions of his later work. Giller's Morey Giller Apartments, Miami Beach, of 1947 features many Wrightian elements, from its asymmetrical, horizontal composition to the incorporation of a crab orchard stone pylon. His favorite of his own designs, the Diplomat Hotel (Hollywood, Florida, 1957–58; demolished), with its circles cut into a concrete dome, reflected Wright's later work like his Annunciation Greek Orthodox Church, Milwaukee, Wisconsin, of 1956.

In the same way that MiMo was a confluence of trends in transportation, lifestyle, even the bright and plentiful packaging of consumer goods, Giller absorbed the forms of his contemporary architects from crinkled canopies to awnings with circular cut-outs like Edward Durell Stone's Museum of Modern Art of 1939. The Diplomat Hotel's hyperbolic paraboloid porte cochere is an example of how the form captured the popular imagination in midcentury, from George Wimberly's Waikikian Hotel in Hawaii of 1956 to Charles F. McKirahan's American Motor Inn in Fort Lauderdale of 1965. Giller's Food Fair supermarkets are as much a monument to the jet age as his civic architecture like the North Shore Community Center, Miami Beach, of 1961, a Roman amphitheater translated into a MiMo vocabulary.

Always an engineering innovator, Giller pioneered many new methods and materials in the Southeast. He conceived of a novel cantilevered truss system in the Ocean Palm Motel (Sunny Isles, 1949) that led to a ubiquitous building type: the double-story motel with catwalks. His Carillon Hotel was the first flat-plate concrete construction in Florida without supporting floor beams to provide the truest glass-curtain wall of its time and place.

When I first met Giller in his Miami office while researching *MiMo: Miami Modern Revealed* with Randall Robinson, I knew he was a gentleman of the old school. His office spoke for the man, from the classic MiMo floating staircase to the chest-height doorknob set in a starburst pattern to his customized lightning-bolt conference table. Conversation with Giller evoked a vanished era when draftsmen in short sleeves and bowties had to use towels to keep their blueprints from curling in the humidity of their un-air-conditioned workroom.

Giller's work is pervaded by the optimism of the postwar era, a sense that subtropical Modernism need not be as severe as its International style counterpart, but instead could go out to play in the Florida sunshine. *Designing the Good Life* is not only a valuable introduction to the work of this talented regional Modernist, it is also a mandate for preservation of the MiMo legacy.

Eric P. Nash
New York, New York

North Shore Community Center, Miami Beach, 1961. Photograph, 2001.

Acknowledgments

Sarah Giller Nelson

I would like to thank my network of friends, colleagues, and family members for their words of wisdom, encouragement, and support. To all those who read early versions of the manuscript—Rachel Griffiths, David Casey, Jane H. Clarke, Beth Dunlop, Mitch Kaplan, John Byram, and Alan Hess—your insights proved invaluable. Thank you. To Robin Hill, your stunning photographs inspired fascinating discussions, and your warmth helped inspire my efforts. To Eric Nash and Randall Robinson, your advice was priceless, your own MiMo book incredibly exciting, and your promotion of my grandfather's work absolutely wonderful.

Thank you, John, Sam, and Honey, for your moral support throughout the highs and the lows. Steve, the floor plans look great. Ira, your dedication to the project, from its inception, has been incomparable. We could not have done it without you.

Finally, I will be eternally grateful to my grandfather, Norman M. Giller, for asking me to coauthor this book. Getting to know him as an architect, a world traveler, a historian, a colleague, and a friend has been an extraordinary experience. I am so proud of all that he has accomplished.

Norman M. Giller, FAIA

This book could not have been written without the support and encouragement of the Giller family and its close friends. Elliott S. Grossman provided essential help during the earliest stages of the project. My children, Ira, Anita, and Brian, were an endless source of encouragement and inspiration.

Ira's architectural expertise often proved particularly insightful. I greatly appreciate my wife Vivian's assistance and support throughout the development of this book. Whether it was making notes, reading and rereading the manuscript, or accompanying me on site visits, she always was eager to lend a hand. My late wife Frances was always active behind the scenes throughout the MiMo years.

I am grateful to Randall Robinson, Eric Nash, and Don Worth for their profound interest in my architecture. Thank you, Robin Hill, for capturing old designs in wonderful new ways.

Finally, I am particularly indebted to Sarah. She spent over two years organizing material, researching, fact checking, and transforming our informal conversations and my virtually illegible notes into a coherent volume. She reminded me of important information, tactfully eliminated unnecessary details, and added essential information from her research. Many of the sections were rewritten a half dozen times or more. She never lost her patience, her energy never flagged, and by the time we got to the last lap, she seemed to know what I wanted to say better than I did. This book is a testament to Sarah's gifts and efforts.

Following page, **Carillon Hotel, Miami Beach, 1957–58 (altered). Concrete accordion-fold façade. Detail. Photograph, 2001.**

ix

Designing the Good Life

Norman M. Giller at
his desk, early 1970s.

A guest arriving at the Diplomat
Hotel, as printed in *Harper's
Bazaar*, December 1959.

Introduction

In the real world Modernism becomes a sliding spectrum, not a pure, single vision. The spirit of the new is shaded and textured by the location, the designer, the culture, leading to a wide family of Modernism.
—Alan Hess, *Palm Springs Weekend*

ARCHITECTURE AND THE MAGIC CITY

In the 1950s, Miami meant glamour, glitter, and excitement. Each winter season, the city filled with sun seekers and starlets wanting to taste the glorious new thrills and spectacular events presented along the Strip. These vacationers stayed in plush hotels, drove Cadillacs and Thunderbirds, spent the day by the pool and the evening being entertained by the era's greats— Frank, Dino, Bob, Judy.

On December 17, 1959, this glamorous world converged at the Café Cristal Supper Club for the gala opening of the Diplomat Hotel and Country Club, a vacation complex I designed. From the entrance canopy's striking form to the lounge's sumptuous silk walls, the resort was intended to evoke drama, exuberance, and luxury. That evening a cocktail party, lavish eleven-course meal, and private concert by famed singer Tony Martin introduced hundreds of VIPs to all the Diplomat had to offer.

The route north from my home on Miami Beach to the party at the Diplomat in Hollywood, Florida, took me along Collins Avenue (Route A1A), passing by many of the other South Florida hotels and motels I had designed. There was the distinctive concrete accordion wall of the Carillon Hotel, dubbed the Hotel of the Year the previous December. Just beyond it was the Golden Sands, my first 100-room luxury motel. A few miles up the road, the sleek, concrete balconies of the Singapore Hotel came into view. I initially conceived of that structure as a hotel-in-the-round.

As I continued northward, Motel Row in Sunny Isles came into view. Here an informal vacation lifestyle reigned supreme. At its southern end was the Ocean Palm, the two-story motel I designed in 1949 that started it all. Beyond it lay what was considered at the time to be the greatest concentration of modern motels in the nation.[1] One after another, the car passed by motels like the Neptune, the Magic Isles, the Bali, the Driftwood, the Carib, the Suez, and the Thunderbird—all of which I had designed.

It was a wonderful feeling to finally pull up to the entrance of the Diplomat Hotel and see it buzzing with activity. I witnessed guests emerging from their cars, awed by the great sculptured entrance canopy. Beyond the plate-glass doors, men in tuxedos and women in ball gowns filled the black, gold, and turquoise Grand Lobby. As the night wore on and I watched guests dance, sip manhattans and martinis, explore the grounds, and admire the hanging staircase, the building truly came to life. It was clear to me then that my architectural career had been building to this crowning moment.

MAGNIFICENT MIMO

Almost fifty years later, at the onset of the twenty-first century, a resurgence of interest in the Diplomat and other buildings I designed after World War II began to develop. In 1999 Randall Robinson, a planner with the Miami Beach Community Development Corporation, and Teri D'Amico, an interior designer, spawned a preservation movement with the coining of the term *Miami Modernism*, or simply "MiMo." Like Los Angeles's Googie, MiMo describes a variety of midcentury structures that epitomized the optimism of the postwar era.

In the last few years, I have regularly been called upon by writers, scholars, curators, and town officials to lead tours, give interviews, participate in symposia, and speak at conferences. Examples of my work have been included in MiMo-related exhibitions and publications. Yet, there are more stories to be told. My granddaughter Sarah, an art historian, and I wrote this book in order to offer a firsthand account of how MiMo—a style, an attitude, and an era—transformed South Florida's built environment in the two decades following World War II. Highlighting twenty-seven of my favorite postwar projects, the book examines the development of MiMo from the unique perspective of someone who helped define it.

EARLY YEARS

Prewar Miami, where I spent most of my childhood, was a sunny, rather quiet southern town. A high school drafting teacher inspired me with the idea of becoming an architect, but the Depression and then the onset of World War II interfered. Postponing college in order to help support my family, I took drafting classes at a vocational school and worked for a local newspaper. In 1939 I was given the opportunity to train six mornings a week with Miami Beach Art Deco architect Henry Hohauser, who happened to be my uncle's friend.

Hohauser, along with others like L. Murray Dixon, Albert Anis, and Roy F. France, helped establish Miami Beach as a modern vacation paradise by designing small hotels and apartment buildings that blended progressive architectural trends, regional needs, and a touch of fantasy. As one of Hohauser's draftsmen, I drew the plans for the dramatic, animated structures whose façades often functioned as advertisements. In order to compensate for the small lot sizes and Depression-era budgets, Art Deco architects often included details like spires, pylons, and tropical ornamentation in their designs. In a sense, the theatrical marquees that crowned the entrances to hotels like the Colony (Henry Hohauser, 1935) were precursors to the expressive porte cochere of my midcentury hotels.

After almost a year of working as an apprentice, I began earning fifty cents an hour. Yet, just as my career was being launched, war clouds began to loom over the United States. Although a high number prevented me from being drafted, I was able to serve my country by working as a civilian draftsman for the military. During the year and a half I spent with the Army Corps of Engineers in Jacksonville, I laid out plot plans for more than seventy-five military training bases in Florida and Georgia. When the V-12 Navy College Training program was created at the end of 1942, I immediately enlisted. The program enabled officer candidates to attend university classes as part of their naval training. Finally, seven years after I had graduated from high school, I was able to pursue an architecture degree.

While in architecture school I became aware of the work of Louis Sullivan (1856–1924), widely considered one of America's first modern architects. Sullivan believed that a structure should reflect the time and place in which it is built rather than historical models. Influenced by the development of the steel-frame skyscraper at the end of the nineteenth century, Sullivan sought to create an American architecture suited to the needs of the modern age. Already possessing modernist leanings from my exposure to Tropical Art Deco and an eye toward the practical from all my on-the-job training, I was particularly drawn to Sullivan's ideas. His tenet that "form ever follows function," or that the exterior form of structure should faithfully express the function within, influenced my approach to architectural design and composition. Sullivan's insistence that ornament should be integral to a structure, rather than applied, began to reshape my understanding of materials. His dismissal of classically dictated notions of symmetry and order encouraged me to experiment with asymmetrically balanced forms. Looking back, I realize that Sullivan's ideas left a lasting impression on my architectural designs for decades.

By 1946, I was married and once more a civilian. With a bachelor of architecture degree from the University of Florida in hand, I eagerly returned to Miami to begin my professional career. But the humble city that I remembered was growing rapidly. Servicemen and -women who had been stationed in Florida began returning to raise families, and tourism was exploding. It was the right time to be an architect in South Florida.

MIAMI-BASED MODERNISM

I have always believed that architecture does not develop in a vacuum; rather, it mirrors the people of its time. The conclusion of World War II ushered in an era of great confidence and prosperity. Millions of veterans, low-interest government loans, the availability of materials, and the evaporation of construction moratoriums spawned economic booms, baby booms, and building booms. Since my midcentury approach to architectural design arose out of and reflected these exuberant postwar conditions, I preferred to use the term *contemporary*, rather than *modern*, to describe my designs. Perhaps *House Beautiful* magazine put it best when it suggested that "to be contemporary is to relax in the twentieth century, to avoid completely the modern strain of straining to be modern."[2] The postwar years were a dynamic, happy period, and my clients and I wanted the structures we were creating to fully embody these "contemporary" sentiments.

In order to meet the enormous pent-up building demand, I relied upon the most efficient and up-to-date approaches to

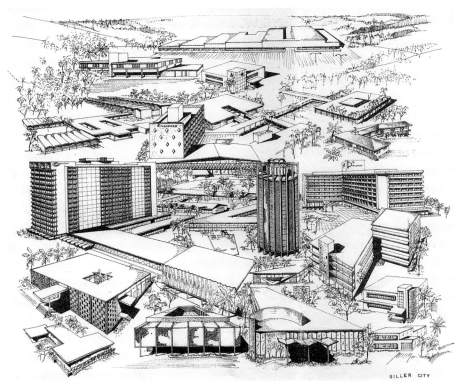

Giller City, 1963. This composite drawing, affectionately named _Giller City_, suggests the quality and quantity of work completed during the firm's first two decades. Drawing by Marvin Schwartz.

architectural design. In the postwar years, this meant drawing upon concepts pioneered by Modern architects like Sullivan, Le Corbusier, Walter Gropius, Ludwig Mies van der Rohe, and Frank Lloyd Wright and using materials and technologies developed during World War II that had been refashioned for civilian use. As a result, my "contemporary" buildings expressed the forward-looking vision shared by many Americans at that time.

Equally important, my designs needed to respond to Miami's subtropical climate. In the days before air-conditioning became common, I experienced firsthand how covered patios, canopies, loggias, porches, and cross-ventilated spaces made living in South Florida more agreeable. The most comfortable buildings of my youth, whether they were in the Vernacular, Mediterranean Revival, or Art Deco style, incorporated features that either took advantage of the climate or protected inhabitants from it. These experiences and my Florida-based architectural training taught me how to adapt my design choices to the characteristics of the region. The first section of this book presents an overview of how technologies, materials, and structures were used to achieve this end. Together, these features endowed my work with a Modernist spirit suited to the area's lifestyle demands.

A description of the twenty-seven projects follows this overview. The commissions are organized in a loose chronological order based on the commission date. Since certain projects were more extensive than others, overlap was common. The text typically describes the distinctive challenges each commission presented and some of my design influences. In addition to photographs and renderings of the buildings, this section of the book includes reproductions of newspaper articles, brochures, advertisements, and other ephemera selected from my personal archives (unless otherwise noted). This historic material seeks to provide a deeper understanding of how my buildings were involved in "designing the good life."

The length, depth, and requirements of the projects commissioned in the 1960s by the U.S. State Department as part of the Alliance for Progress/Alianza por el Progresso program necessitated that I treat this entry a bit differently than the others. Since the eight-year, pan-American undertaking had significant humanitarian goals, my involvement went beyond finding sites, drawing plans, and soliciting contracts. My discussion here specifically addresses how my MiMo design experience influenced the planning of health and educational facilities in Panama, Columbia, Nicaragua, El Salvador, and Brazil. A more extensive account of my involvement with the program can be found in my 1976 book, *An Adventure in Architecture*.

Although *Designing the Good Life* focuses on twenty-seven projects, many more were commissioned during the postwar years. Having always enjoyed the challenge of designing different types of structures, I founded norman m. giller & associates as a general architectural practice. From single-room residential additions to expansive resort communities, no project was too big or too small to accept. This approach served me well: in 1957, *Architectural Forum* magazine ranked my firm the tenth-largest, by project volume, in the United States. In order to help convey the scope of the firm's activities, the book concludes with a listing of significant midcentury commissions and a bibliography.

SHARED VISIONS

As the principal of the firm, I, alone, was responsible for the final design and business decisions. As every architect knows, however, designing buildings is a cooperative process. Ideas often evolved as I worked with my staff of architects and engineers. The contributions of associates like Jan Smit, Sven Speyer, Sylvia Nelson, and engineer Jules Channing were essential to the success of the firm.

Just as architecture is a collaborative effort, this book is the result of a collaboration between Sarah and me. The text developed out of conversations between the two of us augmented, as necessary, by Sarah's research and analysis. The stories are mine; the words are ours. While the book reflects an understanding and interpretation of my work that she and I share, it is written entirely in the first person to emphasize the role of individual experience in the recording of history. As a personal record, *Designing the Good Life* serves to expand current interpretations of postwar Modern architecture, especially the contribution of South Florida. We hope that our words help to inspire others to achieve their own crowning architectural moments.

Technologies

THE AUTOMOBILE

Automotive travel transformed America. The car freed people from the limitations of geography and transportation timetables. With it, people could travel greater distances in shorter periods of time than ever before, and they could do it whenever they wished. Civic, commercial, and domestic spaces were reorganized, and countless industries were generated in order to support and service the car and its passengers. People no longer needed to live close to where they worked or shopped. As superhighways were built, parking lots paved, gas stations erected, drive-in restaurants and theaters popularized, and sprawling housing developments constructed, space was conquered in a whole new manner.

The profound impact that self-powered vehicles had on society captured the imagination of architects and urban planners challenged with accommodating the technology to the built environment. French architect Le Corbusier believed the automobile was the purest, most dynamic symbol of the modern era. For him, the car was the most appropriate model for new architectural forms: "If houses were constructed by industrial mass-production, like chassis, unexpected but sane and defensible forms would soon appear, and a new aes-

Food Fair Shopping Center, South Florida, ca. 1957. Parking lot.

thetic would be formulated with astonishing precision."[1] Le Corbusier's 1921 designs for the "Citrohan" home merged automobile and architecture. Not only is its name a variation on that of the French auto manufacturer Citroën, but the "Citrohan" features a mass-produced, simple concrete-frame design and an integral garage. It was to function, in the architect's words, as a true "machine for living."[2]

In the 1930s, the streamlined shape of transportation machines heavily influenced architectural design. As automobiles became streamlined, so, too, did building types served by and serving the car. The fluid profile, aerodynamic grille, teardrop rear-light housing, and wraparound chrome fenders of the 1936 Chrysler Zephyr or the 1934 Hupmobile inspired the rounded building corners, neon tubing, metallic details, and horizontal speed lines that decorated sleek suburban gas stations, car dealerships, and diners.[3]

When I traveled to the New York World's Fair in 1939, I was able to see for myself how architects and planners were envisioning a future shaped by the car. Like the majority of visitors to the fair, I was most taken by Norman Bel Geddes's "Futurama," housed in the General Motors Highways and Horizons Pavilion, designed by Albert Kahn. The Futurama ride used enormous dioramas and an ongoing audio narration to present America in 1960. For me, the city's vertical orientation, which allowed cars and people to get to places more efficiently,

Polevitzky & Russell Architects, Shelborne Hotel, Miami Beach, 1940–41.

was an impressive, practical solution to the problem of urban congestion. The ground level featured thruways and entrances to underground parking facilities; the second level included elevated sidewalks, safely separating pedestrians from vehicles and allowing for wider traffic lanes below; above these areas, skyscrapers emerged. Once outside the city limits, elevated superhighways and graded ramps enabled uninterrupted travel at top speeds. As the ride progressed, the dioramas grew larger, until finally I emerged into daylight, stepped out of my automated chair-car, and found myself walking on a full-scale elevated sidewalk, futuristic cars below, and the very buildings I had just seen in miniature rising above me. The message was clear—the automobile, a symbol of better living, would comprehensively reshape our lives.

Although the onset of World War II shifted everyone's focus to the war effort, nobody seemed to forget the incredible vision of tomorrow that Futurama proposed. In the postwar years, the automobile fulfilled its promise of becoming an even more powerful instrument of change. The prosperity that millions of Americans experienced during the postwar boom helped make the dream of owning a car a reality. Between 1945 and 1955, the number of automobile registrations in the United States more than doubled.[4] In 1950 alone, over 6.6 million cars rolled off the assembly line.[5] The growth of suburban towns, with their clean, wide, car-friendly roads and their location beyond the reach of buses and streetcars, further encouraged automobile purchases.

As people became more dependent on their cars, and curbside parking became difficult to find, architects and plan-

ners were forced to reconsider how private and public spaces were organized. A car took up much more room than a person, especially when the space required for maneuvering was taken into consideration. Suburban commercial centers began to be designed to incorporate enormous parking lots. Parking lots and garages became standard components of new office buildings. Simply put, if parking was not convenient, the shopper might decide to drive elsewhere or the employee might arrive late for work.

For South Florida architects, the ascendancy of the automobile had an especially important influence on postwar design. The same impulse toward abundance that created Cadillacs with three-and-a-half-foot tail fins and Chevrolets with pounds of surplus chrome fed the exuberance characteristic of the MiMo style. The fin, the grand staircase to nowhere, the 150-foot hyperbolic paraboloid entrance canopy "bespoke luxury, too-

muchness, no-expense-spared largesse."[6] Like Dagmars and tail fins, the expressive details of Miami's postwar structures existed simply to communicate.

Nowhere was communication more important than in the design of the Florida motel. Motels, motor hotels, and motor courts evolved specifically to meet the needs of a car-based lifestyle. These building types developed as clean, informal places for automotive tourists to rest while en route to their destination. Since the initial popularization of automotive tourism in the 1920s, motels had been multiplying along rural stretches of highway where land was inexpensive and abundant. The term, a contraction of *motor* and *hotel*, was first used by architect Arthur Heineman for his Milestone Mo-tel in San Luis Obispo, California, in 1926.[7] Large illuminated signs and unusual thematic adornments were important in attracting the attention of speeding motorists. Ample nearby parking was

also underwent major structural changes to accommodate the unique needs of the car. The Shelborne Hotel (Polevitzky & Russell Architects, 1940–41) was the first modern Miami Beach hotel to feature a long driveway and parking spaces at its entrance. This organizational theme stood in contrast to the streetside entrances typical of the area's prewar Art Deco hotels. The oversized concrete sign that crowned the hotel's roof was designed by Polevitzky to be seen by motorists approaching from a great distance. The formula would be repeated extensively in the postwar years with a dramatic porte cochere often added to attract attention and provide shade. As visitors to South Florida became increasingly dependent on cars, parking garages were added to hotel grounds, as well.

After driving home from a vacation, a trip to the grocery store, or a day at work, car owners needed a place to store their automobile. One of the amenities offered by suburban communities was a new home with an attached garage. Florida's warm climate also made carports a popular option—they were less expensive to build than a full garage and still provided protection from sun and rain. The garage and the carport were typically placed at the front of the home, vying with the front door as the dominant streetside element. While this arrangement made it easy to load up for long trips, bring in the groceries, or get to work when running late, it also pointed to the importance suburbanites placed on mobility and suggested the extent to which the 1950s automobile had become a symbol of status. By the middle of the 1950s, all of the facilities Miami architects like me were designing had to, in some way, accommodate the automobile.

Diplomat Country Club, Hollywood, Florida, 1956–57 (demolished). Entrance driveway.

essential as well. At first, guest rooms were rather bare, but next to each one was a parking space for the traveler's automobile. After a night's rest, it was easy to wash up, get back in the Model A or, later, the Buick Century, and continue down the highway.

The hotel, the motel's older, more urban, upscale cousin,

AIR-CONDITIONING

The development of small, affordable air-conditioning units following World War II converted air-conditioning from a futuristic, commercial novelty into a lifestyle necessity. Initially, the high cost of installing and maintaining an air-conditioning system made the technology practical only for industrial and commercial buildings—or in the homes of the very rich. In the 1920s and 1930s, most people's first encounter with artificially cooled air took place at movie palaces, department stores, and trains. One of the highlights of my Depression-era childhood was escaping the heat at the luxuriously air-conditioned Olympia Theater in downtown Miami.

Although residential air-conditioning systems were developed in the early 1930s, sales took off only in the more prosperous postwar years. After mass-produced, low-cost, window air-conditioning units came onto the market in 1947, the technology, once "just for millionaires," became "integral to the middle-class definition of the American way of life." [8]

In 1948, I purchased two of these window units. Wishing to give my clients an impression that they should associate the designs of norman m. giller & associates with comfort and modernity, I used one unit to cool my office and waiting room. I placed the other unit in the bedroom my then-pregnant wife and I shared in an apartment in southwest Miami. As friends and family learned of our purchase, our once-private bedroom became a hub of activity. With air-conditioned homes still a rarity, friends and family members always seemed to find an excuse to drop by.

One of the first two families to move into the 999 unit Capehart Housing Project at Patrick Air Force Base, Florida, is Master Sergeant George H. James with his family. He is shown explaining the working principles of the new 2¼ ton General Electric Weathertron heat pump, which automatically cools his home in summer and then reverses to heat his home in winter.

As the postwar market for air-conditioning surged, Miami experienced a building boom unparalleled in its history. The ability to control indoor temperatures encouraged people to live, work, and play in the city year-round. The technology facilitated the city's expansion to the west as areas too far inland to receive ocean breezes became attractive to developers.

With the tourist season no longer limited to the cooler months, hotels and motels became even more successful. Neighboring Ft. Lauderdale and Palm Beach experienced similar patterns of growth. By the end of the 1950s, Miami went from being a seasonal town with few full-time residents to a major Sunbelt metropolis.

As air conditioning was transforming the local economy, it was also altering the way South Florida's buildings were designed. The increased demand for cooling systems led architects to reassess window locations and sizes, building elevations, and floor plans. A phasing out of many of the features typical of the prewar, pre-air-conditioned Art Deco style occurred. Expansive, fixed walls of glass replaced heavy stucco walls and narrow casement windows. "Eyebrows," cantilevered sunshades placed over individual windows and doors, evolved into sleek, continuous decorative planes. As designing to encourage cross-ventilation became unnecessary, floor plans took on a newfound flexibility and space was used more efficiently. Offices, lounges, and ballrooms without windows became possible. Lowered ceilings and the removal of front porches, traditionally used to escape hot interior spaces, resulted in more compact home designs. Closed windows and the gentle hum of an air-conditioning unit blocked outside noises and dust, making interiors quieter and cleaner. Due to the extensive impact it had on South Florida, air-conditioning was, perhaps, the single most important technology introduced to the region in the postwar period.

norman m giller & associates
ARCHITECTS

Sebring Hills Housing Development, Sebring, Florida, 1955. Rendering. This air-conditioned midcentury Modern home features a compact L-shape design, an open interior plan, and fixed-glass clerestory and picture windows.

Architectural Elements

CANTILEVERS

A cantilever is a horizontal mass designed to project beyond its supporting walls or columns. Cantilevered slabs supported by six recessed concrete posts, or *pilotis*, were a major feature of Le Corbusier's seminal Maison Dom-ino housing system (1914–15). By the 1930s, architects began using cantilevers to demonstrate the technical bravado of modern engineering. The dramatic overhanging terraces of Frank Lloyd Wright's Fallingwater (Bear Run, Pennsylvania, 1936) are a prime example. Postwar architects used cantilevers to convey lightness, an essential quality of "contemporary" design. Expressive architects like Oscar Niemeyer and John Lautner incorporated cantilevers that extended so far beyond their end supports that they appeared to defy gravity. My hotels often featured large, cantilevered concrete canopies that "hovered" over the entrance as a way to arouse people's curiosity. While a line of columns could be used to support the same amount of load, a cantilevered plane gave a structure an arrestingly modern look.

Beyond serving as a visual element, most midcentury cantilevers served a practical purpose. I used long cantilevered planes to create sleek, continuous balconies in many of the low-rise motels and apartments I designed. Placing the entrances to

North Shore Community Center, Miami Beach, 1961. Cantilevered concrete awning. Photograph, 2001.

each unit from these balconies effectively turned them into outdoor hallways, or catwalks. With the access corridors on the exterior, windows could be put on the opposite walls of the interior spaces, facilitating cross-ventilation.

When placed on the western side of buildings, concrete cantilevered planes also shielded interior spaces from the strong light and heat of the afternoon sun. The most effective sun barriers had a horizontal orientation. A striking example of the use of cantilevers can be found in Alfred Browning Parker's split-level 1953 Coconut Grove home. Parker, a longtime friend and colleague, used deep, overhanging balconies and roofs to create shaded terraces and help distribute breezes, giving an air of delicacy to the grand home.

Vertical sun barriers, either solid or cast in a simple pattern, could also vary the appearance of the façade and provide privacy. The cantilevers were often placed at an angle determined by the sun's direction; the slotted space in between allowed for views and ventilation.

Staircases were another feature particularly conducive to being cantilevered. The treads could be projected out from a thin center column or from a wall. Either design created a dramatic floating-stair effect sure to attract attention. Cantilevered staircases were standard elements in midcentury hotel lobbies, office buildings, and two-story homes, utilized by everyone from Mies van der Rohe to Morris Lapidus. Regardless of how they were used, cantilevers added functional fun and flair to a structure.

Lally columns,
Miami Beach apart-
ment building.

LALLY COLUMNS

A Lally column is a load-bearing structural element made by filling a steel pipe with concrete. Lally columns were developed by mason John Lally in the late 1890s as a fireproof support post. In the event of a fire, the concrete core helps support the load and keeps the metal tube from buckling, while the steel reinforces the concrete if it cracks. Initially the unadorned columns were placed in basements and other areas not generally seen. After Modernist architects began advocating for the honest expression of structural elements, the Lally column became a prominent feature. When supports were necessary along a walkway, groups of two or three Lally columns placed at regular intervals created a sense of rhythm. A flat, heavy carport appeared playful and light when bolstered by sets of thin, cylindrical posts. A "floating" sunshade or a series of metal rings provided a unifying element to a pair of Lally columns. My colleague Morris Lapidus transformed load-bearing Lally columns into decorative "bean poles," using them as design accents to support whimsical tables and bird cages.

Inexpensive and easy to fabricate, customize, and install, the thin column was particularly useful for architects and builders racing to meet the demand for quality postwar housing. Catwalks and carports resting on painted Lally columns can be spotted adorning apartment buildings and homes throughout Miami's postwar neighborhoods. Akin to Le Corbusier's *pilotis*, Lally columns were economical, stylish support structures that provided midcentury architects like me with opportunities to play with proportion, balance, and scale.

Norman M. Giller Residence, Miami Beach, 1951. Intersecting flat roofs.

FLAT ROOFS

Flat roofs became prominent elements in avant-garde residential structures in Europe during the 1910s and 1920s. The flat roof was a feature advocated by Le Corbusier in his seminal 1926 essay, "Five Points Towards a New Architecture," and employed by all of the leaders of the Modern movement.

Flat roofs provided architects with an efficient means of converting the unusable areas under traditionally pitched roofs into living space. Since less material and labor were involved in its construction, a flat roof was less expensive than its gabled predecessor. A gabled roof required a ceiling for the uppermost room, a series of angled roof rafters to support the roof, and material for the roof itself. With a flat roof, the ceiling of the uppermost room and the roof were the same structural element. If level, the roof itself could also function as an outdoor living space. Rooftop gymnasiums and solariums were incorporated into Modernist European homes so that residents could better enjoy the health benefits of exercising, sun bathing, and entertaining in the open air.[1]

Flat-roofed homes were not common in the United States until after the Second World War, when "contemporary" architects were seeking inspiration for innovative, economic designs. The attribute was particularly attractive to designers in California and Florida, where snow loads were not applicable. All of the designs for the Case Study House program (1945–62), sponsored by the progressive West Coast *Arts and Architecture* magazine, included flat roofs, as did most of the homes built by pioneering California Modern developer Joseph Eichler. The lower costs associated with flat roofs made the advantages of modern architecture accessible to millions of forward-thinking middle-class home buyers. South Florida's mild weather conditions and housing needs made the region especially suited to flat-roof buildings.

Norman M. Giller Residence, Miami Beach, 1951. Planter.

PLANTERS

Planters supplied a permanent means of incorporating greenery into the architecture of a home or building. Fixed planters and urns were integral components of Frank Lloyd Wright's Prairie-style house designs. His concern with the relationship between nature and structure held particular resonance with architects in Miami looking to take advantage of the region's year-round green. Art Deco and midcentury architects often framed residential building exteriors with fixed, two-foot-high containers made of stucco, stone, or brick that could be filled with foliage. Functioning as transitional elements between the exterior walls of a structure and their environment, the containers enabled "architecture to mold the landscape" and "the landscape to serve as architectural ornament."[2] By the 1960s, individual planters had evolved into a raised, continuous platform on which a pavilionlike structure was placed. This layering technique provided additional depth to a building's elevation.

With modern and "contemporary" architects designing interior spaces that functioned as interrelated areas rather than distinct boxes, fixed planters became a popular way of dividing a room without having to erect physical barriers. Creating a gardenlike atmosphere inside a large hotel lobby or open-plan living room/dining room/kitchen enabled my colleagues and me to integrate greenery, texture, and color into a space. Whether enveloping exterior walls or defining interior spaces, permanent planters helped seamlessly blend the natural environment with the built one.

Materials

CONCRETE

Concrete is a strong, hard building material that offers enormous flexibility in design. One of the most commonly used man-made construction materials, concrete is produced by mixing cement, water, and aggregate (gravel or rocks) to form a flowing paste. Before it cures and hardens, this paste can be poured into a mold of virtually any shape or embedded with a wide variety of substances.

The abundance of limestone, one of the main ingredients in cement, in South Florida makes concrete an especially attractive construction material for building in the region. Cement is made by heating limestone with clay or sand and then grinding it with gypsum. Local production reduces transportation expenses, making concrete a cost-efficient alternative to other building materials such as brick or steel. Concrete is also fire-safe and highly resistant to wind, water, and insects, concerns in storm-prone Florida.

An early form of concrete was used extensively by ancient Roman and early Christian architects but abandoned during the Middle Ages and Renaissance. During the second half of the nineteenth century, concrete came into use again, though for mostly mundane purposes. In the 1870s, Ernest Ransome in the United States and François Hennebique in France increased concrete's strength by imbedding it with steel rods. Further advances in the fabrication and application of reinforced concrete throughout the end of the century and into the next encouraged architects to explore form in a bold new manner.[1] The versatility and malleability of concrete appealed to "contemporary" architects seeking ways to replace traditional expressions of solidity and balance with dynamic forms that reflected a new preoccupation with weightlessness.

The inclination toward drama and display in Miami at midcentury prompted the city's architects to experiment with concrete's pliability. Cost-efficient yet expressive, concrete enabled my colleagues and me to freely incorporate circles, zigzags, arcs, and ellipses into the structure of our buildings. Flat walls were transformed into undulating planes and simple canopies into super paraboloids. Thick concrete planes floating on angled piers and concrete disks hovering over grand entranceways pushed the boundaries of weightlessness. When properly engineered, the sculptural possibilities of concrete were limitless.

North Shore Community Center, Miami Beach, 1961. Molded concrete "smiles" and "frowns."

Giller Building, Miami Beach, 1955–61, mosaic glass tiles (*left*); Morey Giller Apartment Building, Miami Beach, 1947, crab orchard stone (*right*).

STONE, BRICK, AND GLASS MOSAIC TILE

Combining textures and patterns was particularly fashionable during the postwar period. Architects and designers often broke up stretches of smooth plastered walls with smaller sections of dense, more expensive materials, like stone, brick, or glass mosaic tile. Exterior surface finishes were typically repeated within interior spaces, creating a sense of unity. The durability and organic beauty of stone, brick, and glass mosaic tiles made them excellent, low-maintenance resources, and a preferred means of adding visual interest to South Florida's "contemporary" structures.

Crab orchard stone is a rock mined in Tennessee that was popular in postwar Miami, and a particular favorite of mine. The stone could be cut into bricks and stacked to create a low wall or planter, or sliced into thinner panels to be laid flat on a wall. The textured surface, natural patterns, and slight color variations of polished crab orchard stone panels added a bit of distinction to otherwise empty walls. The material's light, neutral palette contrasted well with the colorful furniture popular in the 1950s and 1960s and was appropriate for use in a sunny environment.

Roman brick is much darker than crab orchard stone, and the exposed side of each sixteen-inch-long rectangular clay block is rough, giving the substance an interestingly varied surface. Since shipping costs from points north made Roman brick more expensive than indigenous stucco and concrete, Florida architects utilized it as an accent rather than a construction material. A wall finished with Roman brick became the focal point of a living room while a Roman brick planter added warmth and depth to the façade of a home.

In contrast to the rich matte surface of crab orchard stone and Roman brick, glass mosaic tiles are bright and colorful. These one-inch-square tiles came in an array of vibrant hues. Tiles arranged in an abstract pattern of contrasting colors grace a large section of the Giller Building's façade (Miami Beach, 1955–61). I always took pleasure in the way the green, yellow, and red tiles shimmered in the Florida sunshine. A few blocks away, two full-height green-glass mosaic tile panels adorn the western face of the Eden Roc Hotel (Lapidus, Miami Beach, 1955). The tiles slowly fade from dark to sea-foam green, recalling the changing depths of the ocean.[2] The lobbies of MiMo resorts and motels often featured fountains embellished with glass mosaic tiles. The play of water and light created an almost magical effect. Although additional accent materials were used in other areas of the country to similar ends, I found that crab orchard stone, Roman brick, and glass mosaic tiles best satisfied Miami's midcentury desire for textural contrasts and natural decorative elements.

GLASS

Glass was extremely important in defining the aesthetic of Modern architecture. In an effort to break with the nineteenth-century tradition of designing dark, gloomy indoor spaces, early proponents of the Modern movement advocated opening up interiors to natural light. From the 1930s onward, the overall window-to-wall ratio rapidly increased. By the time Mies van der Rohe and Philip Johnson were designing homes clad entirely in glass (Farnsworth, Illinois, 1946–50, and New Canaan, Connecticut, 1949, respectively), windows had become one of the most dominant and distinguishing features of Modern design.[3]

Throughout the postwar years, South Florida's architects relied upon various types of glass window systems to expose interior spaces to the natural landscape. Before the advent of air-conditioning, glass jalousie windows commonly served the dual purpose of providing ventilation and light. Developed by the window industry in the 1940s, jalousie windows are composed of small plates of glass, about four inches wide and up to thirty-six inches long, set in a wood or aluminum frame that opens as a series of louvers. Unlike their wooden or metal predecessors, commonly found in the Caribbean, jalousies made of glass allow both air and light to filter into a space. I tended to use glass jalousies to brighten and aerate rooms that lined catwalks. Even when opened all the way, people passing the jalousie windows on the catwalk still had plenty of space to move without bumping into the projected glass.

The development of curtain wall construction techniques

and the popularization of air-conditioning in the 1940s and 1950s allowed architects to incorporate larger areas of fixed glass into their designs. Using a reinforced concrete or a steel-beam skeleton to support the weight of a structure, curtain wall construction enabled exterior walls to act as membranes rather than as load-bearing supports. The transparency of glass made it the material of choice for simultaneously enclosing a Modern building while exposing its interior to the light and beauty of the outdoor environment. Without the climate-controlling capabilities of air-conditioning, however, buildings with fixed-glass window systems would not have been habitable, especially in South Florida. The combination of plate-glass windows and air-conditioning led to a phasing out of glass jalousies, as the jalousies had a tendency to leak cooled air and rainwater.

The ability to use wide expanses of glass as ornament created new possibilities for architectural design, in Miami and elsewhere. Mies van der Rohe's taut, steel-framed, glass-enclosed skyscrapers came to embody the strength, power, and efficiency of corporate America. The design spawned countless imitations, though not all architects and clients adhered to Mies van der Rohe's strict "less is more" philosophy. Glass curtain wall features were considered most appropriate for schools, offices, and public buildings. Variety was added to the glass façade by altering the spacing and size of the mullions or by interspersing transparent glass with opaque or tinted panels. I used this technique to integrate a geometric pattern into the western façade of the guest tower of the Carillon Hotel (Miami Beach, 1957–58).

Large plate-glass picture windows were known for giving living rooms in middle-class suburban tract homes a feeling of airy openness. Sliding glass doors that opened onto backyard patios provided the same effect. The smooth glass counterbalanced the rough texture of stone or brick details. By enabling more natural light than ever to pour into indoor spaces, glass dramatically altered the character of twentieth-century interiors.

ALUMINUM

Aluminum was one of the most efficient, economical mass-manufactured materials available in the postwar years. When it was first isolated in the nineteenth century, aluminum was considered a precious metal, more expensive than gold or platinum. By the early twentieth century, improved manufacturing techniques had increased production levels and lowered its price. Demand for aluminum skyrocketed during World War II, as governments relied on the metal to build planes and machinery. Once the war ended, manufacturers continued to produce the material in abundance. Additional postwar advances in fabrication and finishing methods reduced aluminum's cost and weight, while at the same time increasing its performance.[4] This quality, along with the use of aluminum alloys in the construction of jet-engine airplanes and other aerospace vehicles, gave the metal a reputation for being "a material of the future."

Aluminum was an ideal metal for postwar construction projects. The light material cut transportation costs, eased handling on site, and reduced the weight of increasingly large structures.

A range of forms could easily be created by rolling, extruding, or casting. Lightweight yet durable, aluminum does not absorb moisture, swell, shrink, chip, crack, corrode, or age like similarly priced organic substances. Its resistance to rusting, warping, and fading when exposed for long periods of time to the salty ocean air and blazing sunshine greatly appealed to South Florida's architects.

Not wanting to slow production to prewar levels, postwar manufacturers encouraged the development of a wide variety of aluminum goods and industrial applications. The tubular aluminum folding chair was one of the most prevalent postwar aluminum products, dotting suburban lawns across America. I often encouraged my clients to use aluminum furniture for poolside patios and outdoor dining. Anodized aluminum window frames became popular alternatives to their warp-prone wood predecessors and rust-prone steel competitors. Aluminum-framed glass curtain wall systems considerably reduced the weight of multistory buildings and freed valuable floor space. Aluminum foil insulation was cleaner, easier to install, and more efficient than its fiberglass counterpart. Anodized aluminum could simulate the luster of many other, more expensive metals, including gold, bronze, and brass. Casting anodized aluminum gave a metallic detail a sleek, seamless look. Aluminum's strength, luxe appearance, and cutting-edge reputation made it an obvious choice to use when midcentury architects like me needed to create lavish, "contemporary" environments on a limited budget. Accessible, affordable, and modernistic, the material was well suited to the tastes, needs, and desires of the rapidly growing midcentury modern middle class.

FORMICA

Formica-brand plastic laminate is composed of transparent and printed sheets and is commonly used as a covering for furniture or walls. Formica was an inexpensive, durable, versatile material that revolutionized the commercial marketplace and redefined

Envoy Motel, Hollywood, Florida, 1957 (demolished). Anodized aluminum tables and chairs.

the way postwar interior spaces were decorated. Formica laminate was first manufactured in 1913, though the fabrication of its characteristic decorative surfaces did not begin until 1927. Like many other plastic and synthetic products, Formica came of age in the 1950s. The material's low cost and ease of installation made it particularly attractive to suburban developers quickly trying to meet the enormous postwar demand for inexpensive homes. Continuous, built-in Formica cabinets, countertops, and tables were standard features of the midcentury kitchen. Unlike the ceramic tile it replaced, the material was soft enough to absorb the shock of dropped glasses and dishes yet durable enough to withstand chips and scratches. Like other busy homemakers across the country, my wife enjoyed how simple it was to keep her stain-resistant, nearly seamless Formica surfaces clean. In fact, we still have Formica countertops in our kitchen.

Formica is available in a seemingly endless variety of super-saturated colors, whimsical patterns, and faux finishes. In the 1950s and 1960s, the palette tended to be upbeat and blatantly synthetic. Lime-green, citron-yellow, or powder-blue Formica surfaces coordinated with new, colorful, "time-saving" kitchen and bathroom appliances. Wood-grain Formica coffee and side tables were popular in living rooms, where furniture often took a beating from young children and pets. Typical of the period, the desk I designed for my office is clad in a wood-grain pattern. The simulated finish evoked progress, as well as tradition. The design not only mimics the look of real wood, it improves upon it: Formica furniture does not fade, stain, or warp, and no matter what type of wood it is supposed to look like, the price

is always the same. Formica's durability helped people achieve the more relaxed, informal lifestyle typical of the postwar era.[5] The Formica-filled home was as modern as radar—as were those who lived in it.

Shapes

ANGLES

The diagonal lines of triangles, zigzags, and diamonds convey movement and lightness, qualities that were attractive to a nation obsessed with mobility and motion. The shape was partially inspired by the advent of high-speed delta-wing aircraft.[1] Airplane engineers and designers attempting to break the sound barrier in the 1940s discovered that sweeping wings back obliquely from the fuselage, rather than having them perpendicular to it, lessened wind resistance and increased speed. The United States Air Force Academy Chapel (Skidmore, Owings, & Merrill, Colorado Springs, Colorado, 1954–58) presents one of the most dramatic and literal interpretations of the angular form. Seventeen triangular steel spires make up the building's structural skeleton, distinguishing it from the academy's other rectangular buildings. The spires reach skyward to a height of 150 feet and are wrapped in an aluminum skin. From the outside, the chapel resembles a series of upended fighter planes; inside, the unmistakable outline of a delta-wing aircraft encloses the main altar.

While the delta-wing form was used to suggest motion, the zigzag and the diagonal helped architects incorporate a dynamic sense of liveliness into their structures. Crinkled concrete awnings and slanted concrete columns are common MiMo attributes. The flat roofs of 1950s carports were often supported by a pair of angled Lally columns. Although the carport's heavy slab appeared to be precariously balanced, the diagonal supports were as sturdy as a single, thick vertical column—and certainly looked more exciting. Much of the furniture from this period similarly incorporated angled, spindly legs that seemed effortlessly to support oversized seat cushions and tabletops. The delicacy that slender wooden legs or light steel tubing imparted to "contemporary" furniture distinguished it from its prewar predecessors.[2] Whether used to ornament sacred places or domestic spaces, angles enabled the fashionable architect and interior designer to play lightheartedly with strength and balance.

CURVES

Curves are an eye-catching way of balancing the flat features of a structure. Circles and curves were a standard part of the ornamentation scheme of Miami's prewar Streamline Moderne buildings. The rounded corners, porthole windows, and circular details alluded to the sleek, aerodynamic form of locomotives and ocean liners, symbols of progress and modernity in the Art Deco era.

Carillon Hotel, Miami Beach, 1957–58 (altered). Concrete accordion-fold façade. Detail. Photograph, 2003.

Diplomat Hotel, Hollywood, Florida, 1956–58 (demolished). Circular cutouts along the front façade.

Whereas speed was the essence of the Streamline aesthetic, exuberance was fundamental to MiMo. MiMo architects playfully used concrete domes, disks, arches, and holes in different combinations for expressive effect. The domed roofs of hotel ballrooms had perimeters punctured with circles, and open-air theaters featured arched entrances bisected by large, horizontal disks. Sometimes the forms were fanciful, free-flowing curves, and other times they were lines of circles penetrating a plane. A curvy, covered walkway could give a whimsical, informal air to an outdoor space. Designers would also curve the undersides of horizontal planes. I curved the areas under diving platforms and cantilevered staircases in order to counterbalance the necessary flatness of their top surfaces.

Curvilinear forms were popular in areas outside of Miami as well. Frank Lloyd Wright's circular Guggenheim Museum (1956–59) remains one of the most recognizable structures in the world. Oscar Niemeyer relied on curved concrete colonnades, buttresses, planes, domes, bowls, and arches when designing Brasilia's iconic government buildings from 1956 to 1970. By midcentury, even the austere, Modern designs of Le Corbusier began to incorporate expressive convex and concave forms. The complex curvature of Notre-Dame-du-Haut's sculptural roof (Ronchamp, France, 1950–54) was based on the outline of a crab shell; an upturned parasol inspired porticos, roof structures, and monumental details in the design of Parliament, Secretariat, and High Court buildings in Chandigarh, Bangladesh (1951–65). In a sea of squares and cubes, curves provided unexpectedly daring and dramatic details.

FLUID FORMS

By adding curves to angles, designers were able to create fluid forms. "Contemporary" architects often used curved, irregular shapes to offset rigidly geometric details. The fluid forms were partially derived from the abstract, biomorphic art of Joan Miró, Jean Arp, Henry Moore, and Alexander Calder. The elegant, organic coffee-table that sculptor Isamu Noguchi designed for furniture manufacturer Herman Miller in 1948 typified the cross-over between fine art and industrial design.

The boomerang was, perhaps, the most characteristic fluid form of the period. Boomerang shapes seemed to reaffirm the optimism of a postwar culture where everything was moving forward. Boomerangs and parabolas mimicked the outline of Space Age innovations—jet airplanes and rockets—and could be found on everything from fabrics to Formica to furniture. Sources for the shape included the parabolic curve, the modified delta wing, the stretched and sharpened artist's palette, and the boomerang itself, as imagery from the South Pacific seemed to capture everyone's imagination in the postwar years.[3]

A variation of the boomerang, the free-form kidney shape, proved to be an especially effective configuration for swimming pools. The design served both artistic and practical purposes. A kidney-shaped pool was the stuff of tropical dreams—as striking and exotic as the motel that it enhanced. Since the silhouette had two sections, one larger and one smaller, it was also an ideal form to use when designing a structure that combined a large shallow area and a smaller deep area. After a while, without even realizing it, people come to recognize that the smaller part

of the kidney was the deeper end of the pool and the larger part, the shallower end.

Most importantly, architects and designers used curved, angled, and free-form details in combination with functional necessities. Boomerangs supported rectangular balconies punctured with circular holes. Square holes striated and punched concrete walls in order to make them seem less dense. Aluminum screens were decorated with angled, parabolic figures that seemed to dance in place. Any number of contours could be used in any number of groupings so that the home, motel, or office building would appear exhilarating and inviting.

Chateau Motel, Sunny Isles, 1954 (demolished). Kidney-shaped pool.

Projects

PINE TREE LAKE APARTMENTS

By the 1940s, the format of Miami Beach apartment buildings had become standardized. A two-story rectangular structure containing up to ten units would be erected on a 50 x 130 foot lot. To encourage cross-ventilation, entrances and windows would be placed on opposite walls. Each unit would be about thirty-five feet wide, with the property's additional footage used for setbacks and access. If adjacent lots were purchased, two parallel buildings matching these specifications were constructed on the 100 x 130 foot area. Generally, a double lot provided its owner with up to twenty income-generating apartments.

In 1947, a client asked me to design a two-story apartment building on an odd-sized, premium-priced lot. At 75 x 250 feet, the property was a bit wider and much longer than typical. In order to recoup the higher costs of the land, the building had to include at least twenty-five units. Since this property was, essentially, a lot and a half, I knew that the customary approaches had to be modified. By following the single-building example, I could have squeezed two rows of apartments with an interior center hall into an atypically wide structure. Since this pattern limits unit cross-ventilation, essential in those days before air-conditioning, I had to rule out that option. Instead, I adapted the double-building, double-lot format by placing a single row of units in two slender parallel wings. Like the property itself, each of the apartments was designed longer and more narrow

than standard. With this reorientation, I was able to incorporate three more units than were initially required. The design provided the property owner with a financially attractive investment and would create a comfortable amount of living space for his tenants.

After determining the layout of the property, I then began to focus on generating eye appeal. In order to give the complex a distinctive, unified appearance, I crowned its entrance with a band of upright fins. The detail's configuration also encourages air to funnel through the easterly facing structure. I particularly like the contrast between the smooth, narrow stucco fins and the wide, heavy areas of slump brick bracketing the entrance.

Announcement for the opening of norman m. giller & associates. I opened my first architectural office in the summer of 1946. The timing was auspicious as a major postwar building boom was beginning to reshape South Florida, and architects were in high demand. The firm's inaugural year brought in over fifty clients. By the end of 1947, that number had doubled.

Pine Tree Lake Apartments, Miami Beach, 1947. Front grill detail.

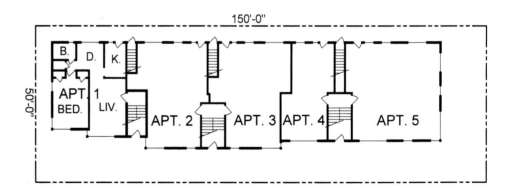

250'-0"

75'-0"

BED.
B.
K.
LIV.
D.
P.

APT. 1 APT. 2 APT. 3 APT. 4 APT. 5 APT. 6 APT. 7

Pine Tree Lake Apartments, Miami Beach, 1947. Lot plan for a 75 x 250 foot property (*above*); lot plan for a 50 x 150 foot property (*right*).

150'-0"

50'-0"

B. D. K.

APT. 1
BED. LIV.

APT. 2 APT. 3 APT. 4 APT. 5

Continuous cantilevered planes run along the flat roof and above the casement windows, further connecting the buildings. The planes are an evolution of the protective "eyebrow" feature commonly found on façades of Miami Beach Art Deco buildings. The Art Deco–inspired interaction of horizontal and vertical elements contributes to the rhythm and balance of the front elevation. By incorporating a dramatic span of fins, replacing painted stucco friezes and other applied ornamentation with exposed brick panels, and elongating the overhanging "eyebrows," I was able to give the building an updated, midcentury modern character.

The fins have caused much discussion. Although to some the grouping resembles the front grille of a postwar automobile, I cannot say I consciously looked at a car and thought to incorporate its forms into a project. At the time I was simply trying to engineer a building that would stand out from its neighbors and exceed my client's expectations. Architecture is, after all, an art, a science, and a business.

Pine Tree Lake Apartments, Miami Beach, 1947. Advertisement, ca. 1948. Furnished apartments were popular with northerners who wished to stay in Miami Beach for the winter season. Typically, a 550-square-foot, one-bedroom apartment rented for seventy-five dollars per month.

norman m. giller a.i.a.
ARCHITECT

MOREY GILLER APARTMENTS

Throughout the late 1940s, a wide variety of building materials became available, and I was anxious to see if I could incorporate the most distinctive ones into my structures. My first opportunity to use crab orchard stone arose when my cousin Morey Giller approached me to design a small apartment building in 1947. The newly quarried stone became an important exterior decorative element. Since the building would sit at the intersection of two streets, I used a two-story, crab orchard stone column to create a focal point at the exposed northwest corner. I placed windows at the corner behind the column, signaling the double height of the interior living room, and used concrete planes to frame and unify the glass and stone feature. The concrete planes double as sun barriers. The texture of the stone gives warmth to the sharp edge and contrasts with the smooth, transparent windows. A duo of load-bearing Lally columns in the center of the entrance façade and a "floating" concrete stairwell at the building's southern end oppose the heaviness of the stone column. A crab orchard stone planter runs along the base of the building, providing additional color and texture to the white, stucco structure.

Anchored by the stone column, the exterior of the building playfully integrates upright and horizontal details. In a nod to Louis Sullivan, the organization of the interior informs the composition of the exterior. While the two-story corner feature indicates the height of the interior space, the elongated "eyebrow" running along the center of the building suggests the division of the first and second floors. The edges of the flat roof and the cantilevered plane extend about two feet away from the walls, helping to keep the interior spaces simultaneously well ventilated and protected from rain and sun. The horizontal line of the overhanging roof, the horizontal line over the first floor windows, and the horizontal line of the planter at the base of the building create a rhythm. The vertical stone column, double-height windows, and Lally-column pairing mix texture, density, and proportion, counterbalancing the horizontal features in a "contemporary" manner.

Morey Giller Apartment Building, Miami Beach, 1947. Rendering by Charles Giller.

Morey Giller Apartment Building, Miami Beach, 1947. The crab orchard stone corner feature (*left*); a pair of Lally columns supports the wooden eaves of the overhanging flat roof (*right*).

Morey Giller Apartment Building, Miami Beach, 1947. Morey's 1948 Cadillac, the first model with tail fins, is parked in front of the two-story, five-unit building.

**Shapiro Residence,
Miami Beach, 1948.
Model.**

SHAPIRO RESIDENCE

None of the rooms of the Shapiro Residence are rectangular, and very few of the walls meet at right angles. The dining room is oval, the Florida Room is triangular, the pantry is hourglass-shaped, the terrace is kidney-shaped, and the living room, kitchen, bedrooms, and bathrooms are irregular quadrangles. These varying geometric shapes balance themselves out, however, making it difficult to tell from the outside the variety of forms to be found inside. One has to look very carefully at the exterior to realize that the walls are not meeting at strict right angles. The property owners, Mr. and Mrs. Herbert Shapiro, came to me wanting to build a "modern house." Like many young war couples, they were beginning a brand-new life in a brand-new world and wanted a home that reflected the fresh ideas of a brand-new generation.[1] I created this unconventional plan to best fit their "contemporary" lifestyle.

The design of the home paired untraditional room shapes with the latest building materials and techniques. The flat roof gave the residence an unmistakably modern appearance, especially in comparison to the older, barrel-tiled roofs of the surrounding homes. I curved the underside of the overhanging stuccoed eaves in order to add a bit of interest to an otherwise plain space. That detail was one of my signature residential elements.

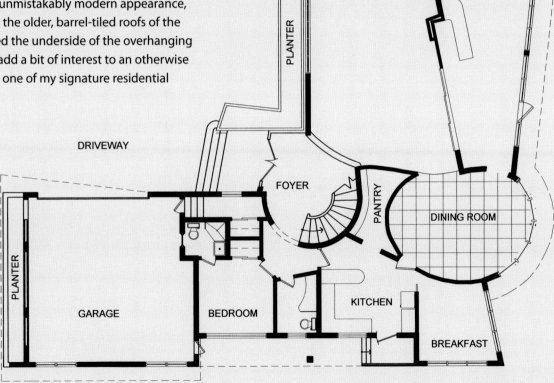

LIVING ROOM

FLORIDA ROOM

PLANTER

DRIVEWAY

FOYER

PANTRY

DINING ROOM

PLANTER

GARAGE

BEDROOM

KITCHEN

BREAKFAST

**Shapiro Residence,
Miami Beach, 1948.
First-floor plan.**

In order to take advantage of the home's beautiful waterfront views, I lined the southern exposure with floor-to-ceiling glass jalousies, just then coming into common use. Since the house was built before residential air-conditioning systems were available, these transparent jalousies afforded the maximum amount of ventilation while allowing the family to enjoy the view. Lined on two of its three sides with glass, the triangular Florida Room served as a transitional space between inside and outside.

The Shapiros spent many years enjoying their progressive home. Not only was the project a fun design challenge, but I also derived a great deal of satisfaction in knowing that I was able to translate the family's needs and desires into a unique residential structure. The current owners were so taken with the home's midcentury modern flair that in 2003 they commissioned Giller & Giller, Inc., to design a MiMo-style addition.

Shapiro Residence, Miami Beach, 1948. The airy Florida Room was an informal living space that allowed residents to enjoy the Florida sunshine from inside their homes. The floor-to-ceiling glass jalousies seen here made the room cool and bright. Popular beginning in the 1940s, the Florida Room was often called a "living porch."

COPA CITY NIGHT CLUB

Miami Beach's Copa City Night Club, a temple to extravagance and glamour, came to epitomize the luxuriant imaginings of postwar America. Dubbed "The Most Fabulous Night Club in the World," the Copa City showcased sought-after performers and hosted famous celebrities in its resplendent, ultramodern setting.

Initially called the Copacabana, the club's first building was damaged beyond repair in a fire in 1947. In the summer of 1948, I was approached by the owner, Murray Weinger, to collaborate with Norman Bel Geddes on a new facility. For over two decades, Bel Geddes had been making headlines with his visionary approach to industrial design and theatrical production. Along with Raymond Loewy and Walter Dorwin Teague, Bel Geddes championed the streamlining technique that gave everything from trains to cocktail shakers aerodynamic profiles and parallel lines of speed.

Although Bel Geddes had proposed designs for theaters, skyscrapers, and homes, he was not a licensed architect in Florida. I was brought in to refine and realize Bel Geddes's concepts, adapt his models to local building codes, and oversee the construction of the project. As an older, more experienced professional with a national reputation, Bel Geddes served as a mentor to me throughout the process. His fearless use of fluid forms, dramatic recessed lighting schemes, and preference for pageantry came to inform some of my own design choices.

Weinger and Bel Geddes wanted the exterior of the new Copa City to be as sensational as the entertainment within it.

To that end, Bel Geddes and I devised a building form that resembled the curved shape of a grand piano. The interior spaces also were wondrously curvilinear. As Mutual Broadcasting Company radio personality Gabriel Heatter proclaimed, "Picture a great big theater—half a dozen other large rooms, a tremendous stage—lighting as new as tomorrow's sunrise, shops of all kinds, rooms for radio and television, and great conventions—yet I can't see a straight wall or column, or a door."[1]

The curving walls of the cocktail lounge gracefully flowed into those of the main foyer, where patrons could purchase corsages or perfumes at the small specialty boutiques. The main theater area was located just beyond the boutiques. Here, guests could enjoy an elegant dinner while being entertained by singers and showgirls. I even included a barbershop by the men's restroom should a fellow need a clean shave at the last minute.

Weinger wanted to make sure that the main theater could host a wide variety of entertainers since singers, dancers, orchestras, comedians, and magicians were to be booked to play the Copa City each season. Bel Geddes and I therefore designed the hall to respond to a range of uses. The rolling stage could be expanded or retracted based on the type of performance being showcased. The entire space was column-free, allowing for unobstructed views of the shows from any vantage point. In order to accommodate crowds of different sizes, I developed a series of hanging partitions that could divide the main area from the perimeter mezzanine. On a slow night, the movable

Copa City Night
Club, Miami Beach,
1948 (altered).
Rendering.

"Nobody ever had to shape materials in those curves before.
Nobody ever had to make light with the magic flickering here tonight.
Nobody ever trained men to put the glass together in the curves they
have had to use here. Nobody ever dared look that far into the future."
—Radio host Gabriel Heatter, opening night broadcast
from Copa City Night Club, December 23, 1948

partitions could be lowered, closing off the outer section in order to give the appearance of a busy club. On a crowded night, the partitions went up, permitting guests to watch the show from the elevated mezzanine.

Weinger demanded that the club be completed in time for the 1948 Christmas season. While press and community members called the project "an impossible dream" (with some entertainers even hesitating to sign performance contracts), the builders heroically managed to complete construction in time for a December 23 grand opening night. For the inaugural bash, 350 different varieties of orchids were flown into Miami. That evening, traffic was jammed for blocks while a steady stream of Cadillacs, Packards, and Lincolns rolled under the huge porte cochere on Dade Boulevard at West Avenue. Hundreds of spectators watched thousands of chic "first-nighters" make their entrance into the club. Inside, Milton Berle, Jerry Lewis, and Dean Martin, among others, dazzled the crowd.

For many years Copa City represented the pinnacle of an exciting, sophisticated Miami Beach style. Eventually, however, the club succumbed to the fickleness of fashion. By the late 1950s, Copa City found itself unable to compete with the newer, larger venues inside the swank hotels along Collins Avenue (a number of which, ironically, I had also designed). After the nightclub closed, the building remained empty for many years. In the 1980s, it was converted into office space. Since the mid-1990s, it has been a self-storage facility. Only hints of the building's original free-form shape remain.

Copa City Night Club, Miami Beach, 1948 (altered). Foyer and shops (*left*); foyer (*below*).

Copa City Night Club, Miami Beach, 1948 (altered). Lounge. Norman Bel Geddes was responsible for the club's interior décor, including the large neon light fixture that illuminated the lounge.

Logo for Copa City Night Club. The front entrance of the Copa City did not have any signs. The building's one-of-a-kind shape was its own corporate identity, as seen here in the Copa's logo, widely used in ads to promote the club.

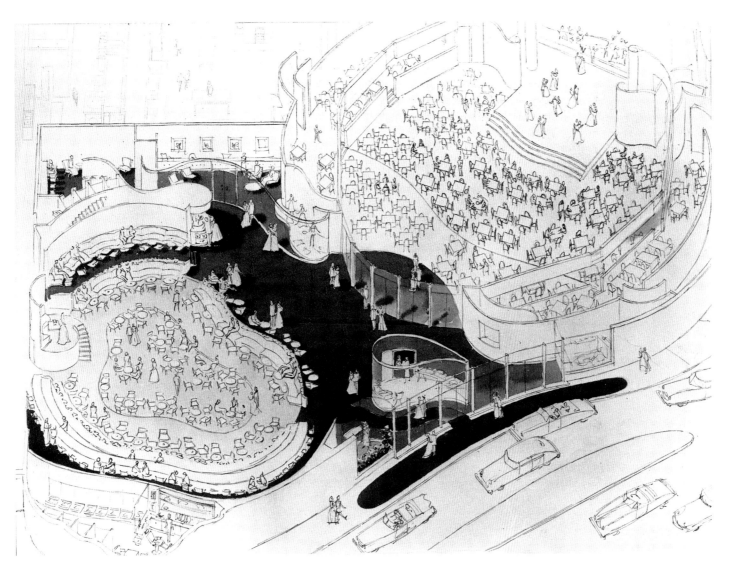

Copa City Night Club, Miami Beach, 1948 (altered). Drawing. The use of air-conditioning at the Copa City contributed to its luxurious atmosphere and unique design. No longer concerned with the natural flow of air through a building, I was able to select materials and organize spaces with greater freedom. A glass-enclosed private balcony reserved for special guests overlooked the main stage. The glass-enclosed front boutique was in the shape of a teardrop, one of Bel Geddes's favorite forms.

MOTEL ROW

On a strip of mangrove-filled Florida beachfront property merely two-and-a-half miles long, postwar architects, developers, and speculators built an extraordinary concentration of modern motels. Between 1950 and 1953, buildings sprang up at a dizzying rate. In two years, five thousand rental units became available. By 1955, over 250,000 guests had visited the fantastic, flamboyant new motels along Collins Avenue/Route A1A in Sunny Isles. Not only did this phenomenon challenge the success of the long-established hotels a few miles south in Miami Beach, but the new-style tourist accommodations fostered a radical change in the American vacationing experience.[1]

It all began with a motel I designed in 1949, the Ocean Palm.

Motel Row, Collins Avenue (Route A1A), Sunny Isles, ca. 1953 (*left*); Ocean Palm Motel, Sunny Isles, 1949. Postcard (*facing*).

OCEAN PALM MOTEL

In 1949, business partners George Berman and Emanuel Seman asked me to design a motel on a newly plotted lot at the southern end of Sunny Isles, an area just north of Miami Beach. State of Florida officials had recently moved Collins Avenue/Route A1A west about four hundred feet in order to stimulate private development in the otherwise empty beachfront area. Berman and Seman's motel site had one hundred feet of frontage on the Atlantic Ocean and spread four hundred feet inland. My clients leased the lot from the owner for six thousand dollars per year in order to build and operate a new type of motel. At that time, motels were just inexpensive, convenient places for car travelers to rest for a night en route to their destination.

Berman and Seman had an innovative idea. They wanted to build a facility with the convenience and price range of a motel

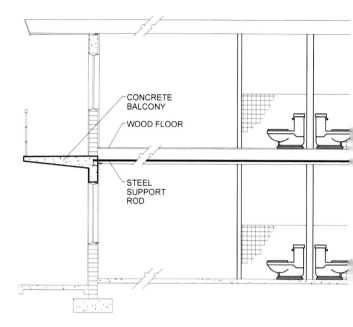

CONCRETE
BALCONY

WOOD FLOOR

STEEL
SUPPORT
ROD

Ocean Palm Motel, Sunny Isles, 1949. Postcard.

that would also be a tourist destination. As far as they knew, this concept had never been tried before. In addition, Berman and Seman believed that the cost of the land was too high to provide a viable economic return on a single-story building, the format motel patrons had come to expect. I then suggested something that, as far I knew, had never been tried before: a *two-story* motel.[1] Thus, we found ourselves faced with two important questions: Would automobile travelers make the motel a destination, and would they be willing to be one flight of stairs away from their cars?[2]

Considering that the motel's backyard was the Atlantic Ocean and that doubling the size of the facility would lower the per-

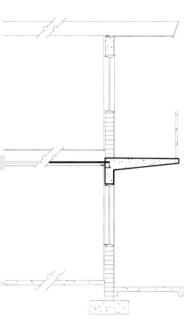

Ocean Palm Motel, Sunny Isles, 1949. Cross-section. In order to give a sweeping, horizontal feel to the motel, the concrete catwalks needed to be column-free. The most direct solution would have been to cantilever the concrete floor of the second story beyond the walls. A full concrete floor, however, would have sent the project over budget. Working with a structural engineer, I developed a method of pairing an interior wood floor with an exterior concrete balcony. This cross-section shows how steel rods placed between the wood floor joists reinforce the concrete balconies. The back-to-back room layout is also evident.

costs and helped to create a more relaxed vacation atmosphere. The floor plan was reproduced in a number of trade magazines and manuals, and it ultimately became an industry standard.[3]

The Ocean Palm Motel opened January 1, 1950, the first day of what was shaping up to be a prosperous new decade. The motel provided clean, new rooms in a beautiful beachfront setting for significantly less money than it would have cost tourists to stay at a hotel. The motel itself, as well as the destination concept that spawned it, proved so popular that an industry entirely new to South Florida was born: the resort motel.[4] We had banked on a location and an idea, and it worked. Soon I began receiving commissions from other motel developers in Sunny Isles, Key West, Jacksonville, Georgia, Atlantic City, and even Montreal. Investment and tourists started pouring into the area. Before long, Motel Row, a "Forty-Million-Dollar Baby," had burst into being.

room cost of the land lease, Berman and Seman decided the risk was worth taking. I was able to make the project even more economically advantageous by developing an extremely efficient floor plan. Rather than organizing two rows of guest rooms along a central hallway, I arranged the rooms back to back with clustered bathroom facilities. Within each cluster, eight bathrooms—four on the first floor, four on the second— shared one plumbing riser. Guests had private access to their rooms via covered walkways on the ground level and via cantilevered catwalks on the second floor. A simple front-office area replaced the formal lobby; long, intimidating hallways were eliminated. The arrangement greatly reduced construction

Ocean Palm Motel, Sunny Isles, 1949. Photograph, 2001. The motel at sunrise. After fifty years, the Ocean Palm continues to attract vacationers to South Florida.

THE RESORT MOTEL

The resort-motel concept catered to the middle class, the sector of the population that grew most during the postwar economic boom. Since the nation's total income was rising twice as rapidly as the population, there was more wealth per person.[1] New white-collar jobs paid for new cars and new suburban homes large enough to accommodate new family members. The universal adoption of paid vacation time made leisure more affordable than ever. After suffering through years of economic hardship and war, the middle class finally was able to start catching up with its aspirations.

Savvy resort motel owners across the country tapped into these ambitions by offering their guests increasingly glamorous surroundings for budget-minded prices. In Sunny Isles, the oceanfront atmosphere was deluxe, the rooms large, and the furnishings rivaled hotel standards. The architecture was described as "fabulous," "flamboyant," "super-modern," and "tropical."[2] Names like the Bali (1951), the Chateau (1954), the Coral Seas (1951), and the Suez (1955) suggested expensive, exotic vacationland fantasies. Spectacular outdoor features helped to distinguish each motel and lure tourists. The Neptune Motel's (1952) sixteen-foot-tall mermaid sculpture competed with the Driftwood's (1951–53) three live flamingos and the Sahara's (Carlos Schoeppl, 1953) plaster camel and Sphinx to attract motorists driving by on Collins Avenue (Route A1A).

While the décor of the cocktail lounge, coffee shop, and private pool area of the motels often reflected their imaginative names, the facilities remained casual. In the era of delicate white gloves and drab flannel suits, this exotic informality had great appeal; it also was a major draw for guests intimidated by the customs and costs of hotels. A survey conducted by the American Hotel Association in 1947 found that many Americans were as "ill at ease" with a "doorman, room clerk, and bellboy" as they were "the first time [they had] to look across a polished desk to see about a loan." In this "strange and different world. . . they [were] afraid of not knowing the right thing to do, the way to act, how to tip, what to say and what not to say to the various employees."[3] The self-service nature of the resort motel eliminated the formalities of uniformed attendants, grand lobbies, and elegant dining rooms, enabling patrons to relax on their own terms. For added convenience, each facility was designed with parking spaces in mind. When the moderate-income family wanted to escape the winter weather, all they had to do was pile in the car and drive to a resort motel in Sunny Isles, where they would be able to experience care-free, oceanside luxury in a setting that satisfied their aspirations as well as their wallets.

"Modernistic architects have been
turned loose [along Motel Row] seemingly with
orders to go as mad as they like to dazzle the eye."
—*New York Sunday News,* **January 25, 1953**

Thunderbird Motel, Sunny Isles, 1955. Brochure.

CARIB MOTEL

The resort motel lifestyle was so appealing that tourists soon began staying at resort motels for weeks at a time. The Carib Motel exemplified the type of facility the Ocean Palm Motel quickly evolved into in order to accommodate these extended vacations. In addition to the thirty-eight conventional guest rooms, the Carib had sixteen suites with living rooms and Pulmanette kitchens. The Pulmanette kitchen allowed the owner to squeeze a stove, refrigerator, and sink into an impossibly small five-foot space and gave the guests opportunities to save money by making their own meals.

Typical of resort motels, the Carib's atmosphere was casual. A coffee shop replaced the dining room, allowing guests to happily leave their ties, jackets, and elegant dresses at home. Since each unit had its own parking spot, it was easy to take the car for a spin on a moment's notice rather than wait for a valet to deliver it. The relaxed environment and Pulmanette kitchens proved especially attractive to parents traveling with children. After a day of splashing in the pool or building sand castles, little ones could be treated to their favorite meal cooked by Mother in the suite's compact kitchen. Both the lower cost and the added amenities of the Carib encouraged its guests to stay longer.

In order to best incorporate these features, I designed the Carib Motel in an H-shape. I connected the two wings of guest rooms with an administrative building. This central building housed the lobby, office, coffee shop, and cocktail lounge and

Carib Motel, Sunny Isles, 1951 (demolished). Façade detail.

Carib Motel, Sunny Isles, 1951 (demolished). Coffee shop. The use of terrazzo floors, paper placemats, stainless steel flatware, and simple chairs helped to create the informal ambience favored by motel guests.

separated the parking section in front from the pool area and ocean in the back. The eastern wall of the coffee shop and cocktail lounge was made of glass, so guests could enjoy the ocean view while they ate and drank. All of the Carib's guest rooms were larger than most hotel rooms in order to accommodate families' needs. Low rates, home-style living, easy parking, complete informality, and the constant glimmer of the Atlantic Ocean drew a continual stream of tourists to motels like the Carib.

Carib Motel, Sunny Isles, 1951 (demolished). Exterior view. The finlike sun screens added flair to the design and provided protection from the sun (*above*); ground-floor plan (*right*).

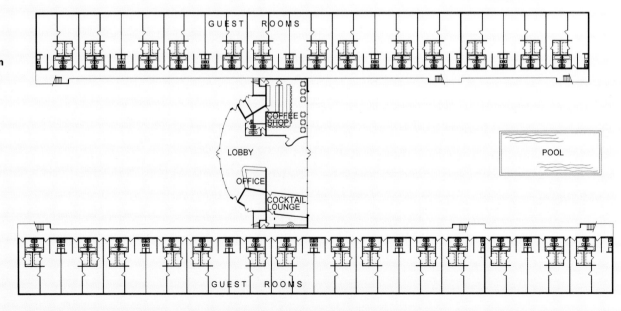

GUEST ROOMS

COFFEE SHOP

LOBBY

OFFICE

COCKTAIL LOUNGE

POOL

GUEST ROOMS

DRIFTWOOD MOTEL

The Ocean Palm and the Carib were just two of the sixteen motels I planned between 1949 and 1952. Based on the experience I gained from these commissions, I soon was able to formulate a set of basic guidelines for the building type. A modern approach to balance, continuity, color and texture, and scale proved to be the most important factor in a successful motel design. Since asymmetrically arranged elements best attracted motorists, the building had to convey a sense of movement and spontaneity. Yet, there also needed to be order in the overall effect. Continuity between interior and exterior elements created a comforting rhythm and memorable identity. Color schemes and textural elements affected mood and had the power to make a room seem spacious and pleasant or small and uncomfortable. The "human factor" in architecture was also significant. As the motel is a structure for human beings, everything had to be scaled in proportion to them. While it

Driftwood Motel, Sunny Isles, 1951–53 (demolished). Photograph showing the façade's intersecting planes in the Florida sunshine. The original wing is to the left.

was crucial that a motel be eye-catching, too much height and grandeur could be as bad as none at all.

When Aaron Courshon and Paul Pollack wanted me to add sixty rooms and enlarged, air-conditioned public areas to the fifty-room Driftwood Motel I had designed for them in 1951, I relied on principles like these to create an enticing, attractive structure. The original facility was a single, two-story building similar in size and shape to the Ocean Palm. Incorporating the additional rooms without spoiling the character of the older building would be challenging. I needed to be an artist and an engineer every step of the way.

I ultimately decided to place a new wing parallel to the first building and connected the two branches with a 65-foot long undulating lobby. I raised the lobby about one-half story, creating just enough space beneath it for cars to pass through to reach the parking area in between the two wings. The floating walkway recalled the futuristic pedestrian overpasses from the 1939 New York World's Fair Futurama display I had seen as a teenager.

The lobby is the first step in selling a guest on the quality of the motel's services and environment. With air-conditioning allowing me to manufacture the climate, I enclosed the room in non-load-bearing walls of glass that enhanced the section's

Driftwood Motel, Sunny Isles, 1951–53 (demolished). Photograph, 2001 (*left*). In 1954, *Detroit Free Press* reporter Arthur Juntunen visited two Detroit couples, Paul and Rosemary Dallas and Bob and Rita Camerlengo, vacationing at the Driftwood. These pictures appeared with his story (*right*).

HORSEPLAY at the pool is common at Motel Row. Here Paul Dallas and Bob Camerlengo (in water) take plunge, shoved playfully by Rosemary and Rita.

SHUFFLEBOARD is popular sport at Driftwood. Bob (left) and Paul watch critically as Rosemary plays. Rita awaits turn to display her skill at the game.

IN CHANGE of pace from gay life of pool and ocean beach, Rita (left) and Rosemary visit live flamingos displayed in pond at front of motel.

AT DRIFTWOOD, life is in the hands of Lifeguard Don Anaston, U. of Miami student. To prove it, he hoists Rosemary and Rita off ground.

MOTEL LIFE means home life on beach. Bob, playing chef-waiter, serves breakfast to Rita, Rosemary, Paul. Apartment was on edge of pool.

Driftwood Motel, Sunny Isles, 1951–53 (demolished). Postcard. The entire structure glowed at night, beckoning tourists. Despite the success of motels like the Carib and the Driftwood, almost all of the original low-rise buildings have now been replaced by soaring, forty-story luxury condominium apartments and hotels.

sleek, featherweight appearance. From the windows of the air-conditioned space, guests could see the swimming pool, the play area, the beach, and the Atlantic Ocean. When lit at night, the glass lobby looked like a beacon suspended in midair.

The frame of the curved, hovering lobby ended at a decorative four-story series of intersecting vertical planes. Playing with volumes and textures, I adorned one of these areas with rough, Roman brick and the other with smooth stucco. The Driftwood's sign ran along the top of this tower, and the motel entrance was at its base. The owners placed an enormous piece of driftwood on the larger, smoother plane, further directing guests to the entrance. I also repeated on the second wing the vertical concrete sun barriers and grid from the façade of the original building.

The design of the Driftwood Motel was also influenced by one of the most revolutionary technologies of the day, a television. Since TV was a new, excitingly modern medium, television sets were an attractive guest amenity. With the high price of early sets preventing Courshon and Pollack from purchasing one for each room, I designed a common area off the lobby where guests were able to watch their favorite programs. Continuing the motel's theme, the owners decorated the TV Room and other public areas with small pieces of driftwood.[1]

Driftwood Motel, Sunny Isles, 1951–53 (demolished). TV Room.

Thunderbird Motel,
Sunny Isles, 1955.
Postcard.

"The Thunderbird will be ultra-modern in its every line and
decor. From the low-sweeping front canopies to its rich two-deck
interior lounges, it is an Arabian Night's dream come true."
—*Miami Beach Sun*, August 21, 1955

THUNDERBIRD MOTEL

"Thunderbird to Be Tourist Dream" read the headline of a 1955 *Miami Beach Sun* review. The owners of the Driftwood, Aaron Courshon and Paul Pollack, hired me to design a resort motel more lavish than its predecessor but not overly extravagant. My interpretation of their needs suggested a complex that was spacious yet could accommodate more amenities and guests than was typical in a facility of its price range. I envisioned guests entering a large, glamorous lobby and then being directed to one of 160 ocean-view rooms. While the children were busy in the play area or splashing in the kiddie pool, parents were visiting the massage or steam rooms or solarium. When it rained, there would be two television rooms, and when it was sunny the cabana club would welcome poolside guests. A coffee shop, cocktail lounge, and dining room allowed patrons to indulge almost any time of the day. As Courshon and Pollack requested, the Thunderbird would reach new heights in luxury on Motel Row.

In order to incorporate all of these elements, I devised a U-shaped building featuring a four-story guest-room tower. The design benefited from modern innovations, such as central air-conditioning and elevators, not generally found in motels at the time. The lobby spanned the entire front of the property. Its

Thunderbird Motel, Sunny Isles, 1955. Advertisement. The aerial view of the motel seen in this advertisement shows the guest tower's sawtooth-pattern floor plan. This layout, common in Miami Beach, provides private, unobstructed views from each guest room.

OPENING DECEMBER 1st
A Masterpiece in Design and Elegance

Just a Few of The Thunderbird Advantages, Unmatched Anywhere!

- Centrally Air-conditioned & Heated, Individual Room Control
- 2 Outdoor Swimming Pools— Olympic size & Play Pool
- 300 Feet of Private Beach & Cabanas
- Swedish Massage & Steam Rooms
- Oceanside Coffee Shop
- Main Dining Room— Finest Foods & Service
- Cocktail Lounge
- Adult TV & Cinema Theatre
- Children's TV & Cinema Theatre
- Finest Equipped Solarium
- Private Kitchens available
- Beauty and Hairdressing Salon— Barber Shop
- Poolside Cocktail Bar
- Tennis Courts—Table Tennis— Shuffleboard
- Running Ice Water in Each Room
- Englander Foam-Rubber Mattresses
- Every Room Faces the Ocean
- Every Room has Private Terrace
- Every Room Scientifically Sound-proofed
- Elevator Service— to Beach or Lobby
- Private Bath & Phone in Each Room
- Supervised Children's Play Room, Nursery
- Golf Range—Boat Docks— Fishing on Premises
- Parking Free at Your Door
- Planned Entertainment: Movies, Barbecues, Dancing, Beach Parties, Moonlight Sails, Entertainment

THE WORLD'S MOST LUXURIOUS

COMPLETELY AIR CONDITIONED & HEATED

THUNDERBIRD RESORT MOTEL

NOW ACCEPTING RESERVATIONS!

FROM $4 DAILY PER PERSON DOUBLE OCC. TO DEC. 15

WRITE, WIRE or PHONE THE THUNDERBIRD DIRECT Miami Beach, Fla. 816-4521

LUXURY WITHOUT EXTRAVAGANCE

On The Ocean At 184th St., Miami Beach, Fla.

sloping, ranch-style roof and brick façade details alluded to the motel's western theme. The ceiling of the lobby followed the angle of the roof, making it three stories tall in some sections and two stories in others. Since the entire facility was air-conditioned, I focused on using windows for light and ornament, rather than ventilation. The lobby's ultramodern chandelier, stylish interior décor, and high ceiling made an impressive first impression.

In order to balance the front building's asymmetrical shape, I situated a four-story tower of guest rooms at the narrower, left edge. As with the Ocean Palm, the cost of the land necessitated that the building be expanded upward. Since the owners were concerned with the public's acceptance of a four-story motel, I added elevators and planned the tower so that from the highway side it appeared to be a two-story building. The west wall of the structure was solid, because it faced the afternoon sun. On this blank wall, I placed an enormous Thunderbird sign that minimized the building's height and could be seen by motorists over a half mile away.

Instead of placing another four stories of guest rooms on the south side of the site, I designed a small, two-story building to house the dining facilities and cabana club. This arrangement contributed to the luxuriousness of the resort by giving

Thunderbird Motel, Sunny Isles, 1955. Upon entering the motel, guests found themselves standing in a grandiose, multistory lobby. The large chandelier crowned the space. A floating staircase at one end led guests to a mezzanine overlooking the main floor. Planters and plate-glass walls helped blur the distinction between inside and outside.

each guest an unobstructed ocean view from his or her private balcony and a bit more elbow room on the property. The lobby spanned the two wings. Behind it were two pools, a cocktail bar, and areas for sunbathing, games, and special events. Parking was located along the perimeter of the property. Advancing the original resort motel concept, the owners also offered valet parking services. When it was built, this four-story fantasy was the tallest oceanfront motel in the country.[1] From the Ocean Palm to the Thunderbird in only six years was quite a development!

Thunderbird Motel, Sunny Isles, 1955. Brochure.

Sebring Hills Housing Development, Sebring, Florida, 1955. Rendering.

SUBURBAN HOUSING

While the South Florida tourism industry was fervently catering to the ambitions of its middle-class visitors, South Florida's suburban housing industry was diligently helping its middle-class residents and returning veterans afford the American Dream. Owning one's own house had always been a part of this dream, and during the 1950s more people were able to own a home than ever before.

Much of the rise in home ownership was due to the passage of the Servicemen's Readjustment Act of 1944, better known as the GI Bill of Rights. As early as 1942, the Franklin D. Roosevelt administration was anticipating the need for jobs and housing for approximately 15 million servicemen and women who would return home from overseas when the war ended. This piece of legislation had a profound effect on American society in the postwar years. In addition to entitling veterans to unemployment benefits, job training, and four years of college tuition, the GI Bill provided loan guarantees to purchase a house or start a business. The subsequent social mobility made the features of middle-class status—home ownership, a college degree, and a white-collar job—accessible to millions. The loans fueled a housing boom that reshaped cities across the country. In fact, the challenge of building in the years following the end of World War II was keeping up with the tremendous demand.

With so many people needing places to live, I, along with other architects, developers, and builders, had to devise methods for building as many inexpensive units as possible in a very short time. Constructing homes of a standard design on site in an assembly-line fashion was one way that this was accomplished. Real estate developers Levitt and Sons perfected the technique with the construction of the first truly mass-produced suburb, Levittown, New York (1947–51). The approach was widely adopted in the postwar years. Using their system, the average contractor could put ten foundations and footings in place in one day. While the walls were being erected on those residences, the next series of ten foundations could be laid. Then

TYPICAL BUNGALOW IN A GROUP being built for veterans by the M. Giller Co., to be sold veterans for approximately $8,900.

Very few private homes or apartment buildings were built during the Great Depression (1929–39). Throughout the early 1940s, all available materials and labor were required to further the war effort. After the war ended, developers in South Florida began building homes in record numbers—50 units, 100 units, 250 units, 500 units, over 1,000 units—in order to end the housing famine. In 1947, I designed a 1,000-unit housing project for my father, real estate broker Morris Giller. Newspaper clipping ©*The Miami Herald*.

"House with Four Faces," Miami, 1949. Exterior view. I placed this unit's front door in the center, underneath the overlap of the two flat roofs. The adobe brick wall is exposed on the interior as well as the exterior, adding texture and color to the living room.

masons, electricians, plumbers, carpenters, and roofers would progressively move from house to house, completing groups of homes at the same time by using the same methods and pool of materials.

The speed with which these dwellings were erected necessitated that they be bare bones, practical, and almost identical in appearance. While this construction technique fulfilled the urgent need for housing, it also created a physically homogeneous environment that consumers soon found unappealing. Convinced that a home with individual character and good design could be built as economically as the boxy, conventional, low-cost homes on the market, I devised the "House with Four Faces" in 1949. By paying close attention to the construction details, I was able to design a relatively large structure affordable to those with moderate-sized pocketbooks. The home's floor plan was based on standard material sizes, with the dimensions of the rooms corresponding to the size of the lumber commercially available. This way, the homeowner avoided paying for unused material and extra labor. I then clad this one basic floor plan in four different exterior shells. All of the models featured two bedrooms, a carport, a sloped roof overlapping a flat roof, a raised entryway, and an adobe brick accent wall. By simply altering the location of the front door and the carport, varying the carport's supports, and modifying the angle or length of the sloped roof, I was able to create four distinctive-looking homes. After convincing the subcontractors to use new, lower-cost building methods and securing Federal Housing Administration (FHA) financing, the developer was able to sell these homes for approximately $9,500.

Sunday, June 12, 1955   THE MIAMI HERALD   3-G

For R&K Construction Co.

Giller Designs Unusual Small Home

The problem of designing a small home which can be built at comparatively low cost yet with custom home individuality is one which has presented a challenge to many architects.

For it seems the instant design departs from absolute conventional styles, the construction costs skyrocket.

Builders, generally, prefer to stay with a strictly rectangular design — avoiding odd shapes, since extra corners always mean higher costs.

Norman Giller, Miami Beach architect more noted for his motel and commercial work than anything else, has tried his hand at small homes — designing two for the R&K Construction Co.

In the home illustrated here Giller has retained a basic rectangle in design yet avoided the box-like appearance of a conventional rectangular house.

This was principally achieved by carrying the roof line in a gradual slope down from the ridge of the house across the car porte.

He has walled the living area with tiers of jalousied windows extending upward from the floor.

He has provided a screened patio off the dining area and carried the masonry front wall across in front of this patio, both to maintain design unity from the front and to afford privacy.

A basket weave fence has been built in the gap between the car porte and side of the house shielding the large side yard from the street.

The home is also equipped with built-in equipment in the kitchen and large jalousied windows in all bedrooms.

The R&K homes, being sold on FHA financing only, are located at NW 130th st. and 22nd ave.

NOTE LONG SLOPING ROOF LINE OVER CAR PORTE

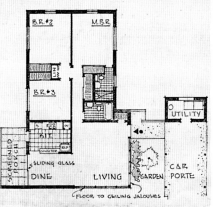

R&K HOME IS BASICALLY RECTANGULAR

Throughout the 1950s and early 1960s, I designed similar residential developments in communities across Florida, including Cocoa, Ft. Lauderdale, Key West, Punta Gorda, and Sebring. Many of these homes have remained occupied into the twenty-first century. Newspaper clipping ©The Miami Herald.

Coral Way Village, "The Magic Home" Model, Miami, 1954. The combined living room/dining area. The three-bedroom residences were only about 1,300 square feet. In order to increase the apparent size of the unit, I avoided organizing the living room, dining room, and kitchen into separate cubicles, an approach favored by Modern architects. Floor-to-ceiling glass jalousie windows provided ventilation and contributed to the openness of the space. In a 1954 *Miami Herald* newspaper article, this model was lauded for its "airy roominess."

For the 1,000-unit Coral Way Village housing development I designed for Gene Fisher and Arnold Rosen of F&R Builders Inc. in 1954, I devised additional ways of incorporating variations into basic home models without sacrificing time or going over budget. The five standardized floor plans could be combined with a choice of ten exterior styles. The homes could be painted white, lime-green, or blue; incorporate planters made of slump brick or painted stucco; include a screened-in porch or an open patio; and have a flat, sloped, or angled roof. For an additional four hundred dollars, a carport supported on brick columns, vertical Lally columns, or V-shaped Lally columns could be added to the front or the side of the dwelling.

F&R wanted to sell these homes for ten to twelve thousand dollars. In order not to price them out of the market but still appeal to buyers who were faced with many choices, I also made sure to incorporate easily modifiable interior details. "The Magic Home," for instance, included a large closet off the master bedroom with rough plumbing installed, giving the homeowner the ability to convert it into a second bathroom.

Whereas prewar suburban towns were havens for the wealthy, postwar developments like Coral Way Village enabled the upwardly mobile middle class to take advantage of the clean air, healthy atmosphere, and uncrowded streets char-

Coral Way Village, "The Magic Home" Model, Miami, 1954. The kitchen featured a dishwasher and garbage disposal, newly available appliances generally not included in homes of this price range. F&R was the predecessor to the Lennar Corporation, one of the largest home-building companies in the United States.

Coral Way Village, Miami, 1954. F&R had purchased 223 acres of land just off of Coral Way, a major road in the southwest part of Miami-Dade County. When the developer approached the FHA to guarantee the mortgages, the FHA initially turned them down, arguing that the project was too far from the center of Miami to garner many sales. As this line of people waiting to see the model suggests, however, F&R proved correct in its calculations. Nowadays, it is hard to imagine that this area was ever on the outskirts of the city (*above*); advertisement (*right*).

acteristic of suburban neighborhoods. The combination of mass-production construction methods, low interest rates, tax breaks, and government-backed loans made owning a home outside the city more affordable than renting an urban apartment. Indeed, by 1955, four thousand families a day were leaving the city for the suburbs.[1] With models named "The Villager," "The Suburbanite," and "The Success Model," merchant builders like F&R could sell the American Dream to South Floridians for payments as low as $69 per month. Today, the lure of a much less modest suburbia continues to redefine American life.

Homestead Air Force Base, Homestead, Florida, 1956–58. Rendering, aerial view.

MILITARY HOUSING

The residential communities I planned for the armed forces at Homestead Air Force Base in Miami, Patrick Air Force Base in Cape Canaveral, and the U.S. Naval Air Station in Key West built upon the success of the earlier private-sector housing developments. While home design was an important part of these military projects, they also required that my firm plan virtually self-sustaining communities for thousands of people. Roads and sidewalks, parks and landscaping, and plumbing and electrical distribution all had to be integrated into the housing scheme.

Following the conclusion of World War II, the military found itself faced with a complex housing shortage. The onset of the Cold War created a need for a large peacetime fighting force, the first in U.S. history. As the armed services became increasingly dependent on technology, the retention of highly skilled specialists also became important. Military officials soon recognized that high-quality homes for military families were crucial for the continued protection of the country. Not only did servicemen and -women need to be on duty on a moment's notice, but attractive family housing options were good for morale, helping to entice and retain the most talented personnel. Budgetary constraints, however, initially limited the scope and quality of residential construction projects.

The turning point came in 1955 when Congress passed the Capehart Housing Act, legislation sponsored by Senator Homer E. Capehart that enabled the armed services to build homes without relying on taxpayer dollars. Under the Capehart program, residences were constructed and financed by private developers on land owned by the government. This arrangement avoided the bureaucratic red tape typical of public construction projects and allowed the dwellings to be larger and of higher quality than if their costs were part of the federal budget. The Department of Defense purchased and managed the units once they were built, paying the privately held mortgages with the housing allowances allocated to the personnel renting each home. With the Department of Defense owning the residences, military families could not be gouged, a problem they often encountered while renting off-base housing. By the early 1960s, more than 115,000 Capehart family housing units had been built.[1]

Although the Capehart legislation did not include specific style guidelines, the residences were overwhelmingly "contemporary" in design. Since "contemporary" implied improvement, comfort, and an overwhelming faith in tomorrow, it came as little surprise that a cutting-edge, technologically driven military would want its residential communities to express America's progressive and newly informal lifestyle. An affiliation with modernity was especially important to the U.S. Air Force, created in the 1940s and eager to distinguish itself from the older, tradition-bound branches. Due to the importance of air power in World War II and the Korean War, the U.S. Air Force was considered by many to be "the ascendant military force of the postwar era."[2] By blending progressive architecture with a postwar military agenda, the Capehart communities could go

Capehart Family Housing, Key West Naval Air Station, Key West, 1960–62. Rendering. Duplex units gave renters the same sense of privacy they would find in a freestanding house. Shared walls and driveways saved space, materials, and construction time (*above*); floor plan of a four-bedroom duplex unit (*right*).

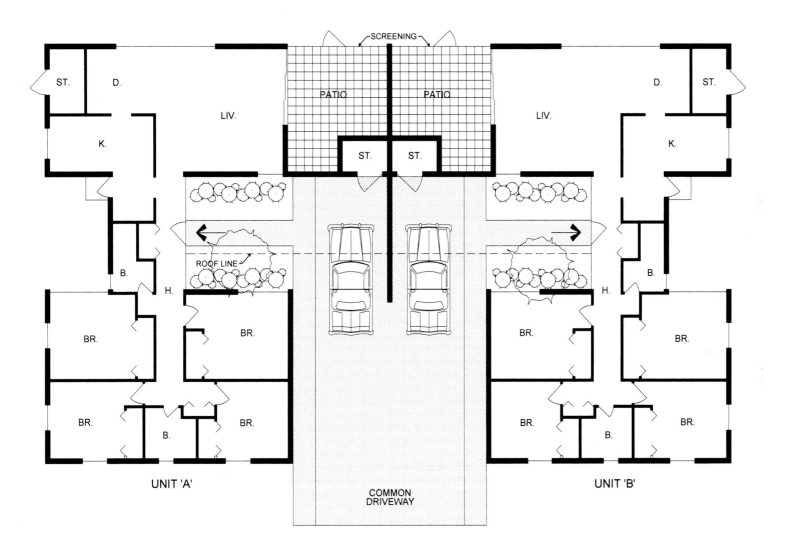

ST. D. LIV. SCREENING PATIO PATIO LIV. D. ST.

K. ST. ST. K.

B. H. ROOF LINE H. B.

BR. BR. BR. BR.

BR. BR. BR. BR.
B. B.

UNIT 'A' COMMON DRIVEWAY UNIT 'B'

beyond simply alleviating a housing shortage; they would permit service personnel to serve their country by living the type of forward-looking lifestyle they had vowed to defend.

Having spent the postwar years designing hundreds of "contemporary" suburban homes in South Florida, my firm found itself well positioned to accept commissions from base officials in Homestead, Cape Canaveral, and Key West. As with the private-sector housing developments, I based the design of the military accommodations on a set number of well-thought-out floor plans and modified their exterior elements. All of the units were constructed of concrete block and stucco, with adobe brick accent walls. Many of the architectural features functioned as both structure and ornament. Concrete awnings supported by pairs of Lally columns shaded entranceways and carports. The columns contributed to the rhythm and balance of the structures' exteriors. Angled flat roofs with wide overhangs imparted the residences with a modern appearance and protected their interiors from the sun and the rain. The long, sleek roof lines gave the houses a streamlined look particularly appropriate for buildings occupied by jet-age fighter pilots. I framed the exterior of the homes with brick planters, and, in a few of the models, I punched holes through the front concrete awnings to allow for the growth of palm trees. These features provided a gradual transition from outside to inside, and between natural and architectural. Variations in color, roof design, carport configuration, and materials resulted in many different home styles.

The military specifically required that the appearance of the

homes reflect the status of the occupants. The higher the officer's or enlisted man's rank, the larger and more elaborate the unit. Most homes had three bedrooms, though there were four- and two-bedroom houses available as well, depending on the serviceman's position.

Regardless of their size, the homes were designed to feel light and airy. By placing screened patios off the living room/dining room areas, I was able to extend the living space to the outdoors. Sliding glass doors, floor-to-ceiling glass jalousies, and plate-glass windows allowed the bright Florida sunshine to stream into the interior areas. The open-plan organizational scheme made the 960- to 1,535-square-foot homes seem larger and encouraged residents to enjoy a more relaxed, suburban-style way of life.

HOUSE #6A

norman m. giller & assoc.
ARCHITECTS ~ ENGINEERS

HOUSE #2·C

Capehart Family Housing, Homestead Air Force Base, Homestead, Florida, 1956–58 (destroyed). Renderings. Each of the 1,255 homes originated as one of seventeen basic plans. Variations in exterior elements resulted in over one hundred different styles in the community.

norman m. giller & assoc.
ARCHITECTS ~ ENGINEERS

HOUSE #7B

"There is nothing more vital or pressing
in the interest of morale and the security of America
than proper housing for our armed forces."
—Louis A. Johnson, U.S. Secretary of Defense, 1949

When considering the comprehensive plan for these communities, I had to envision how the different structures and their occupants would interact with one another. Overall, the layout of the military developments resembled their civilian counterparts. By the mid-1950s, the geography of these communities had become well established: uniformly set-back homes were situated on long blocks uninterrupted by cross-streets; and wide, curvilinear streets and cul-de-sacs ensured that traffic through the neighborhood would travel at safe, slow speeds. In order to maintain the ideal density for the military communities, single-story homes were constructed three to four per acre. Landscaping added shade and variety. When selecting foliage for the Key West base, I had to be particularly concerned with the island's acidic soil. Coordinating paint colors were chosen for each house's exterior. A tropical palette of white, yellow, light-green, and light-blue was popular at the time.

Although the basic components of the three armed-services projects were stylistically similar, each community had its unique needs. Homestead AFB was part of the Strategic Air Command (SAC), which was responsible for both early warning of and defense against missile and long-range conventional attacks. In order to fulfill this mission, the SAC had planes in the air twenty-four hours a day, seven days a week. Due to this schedule, SAC staff worked long, irregular hours. Air force officials needed their pilots and personnel to live on the base so, if needed, they could become airborne in minutes.

With planes flying at all hours of the day, the noise made sleeping difficult. The simplest solution would have been to

Homestead Air Force Base, Homestead, Florida, 1956–58 (destroyed). Photograph, 1958. All of the sewage lines from the homes led into this enormous, concrete catch basin. From there, one large line ran to the sewage treatment plant on the main part of the base. Four cranes were needed to lower the eighty-ton, precast concrete structure into the hole. The scale of the housing development made such a large catch basin necessary.

keep the windows of the homes closed and allow the hum of an air-conditioning unit to block some of the sounds of the jet engines. Unfortunately, U.S. Air Force regulations mandated that only heating could be installed in their housing units. Homestead's long, hot, humid summers and warm winters made heating systems impractical. For months, the base's commanding officer, Colonel James W. Twitty, and I tried to convince the air force to make an exception to this policy, and for months our request was denied. The situation put the entire project on hold.

Then, in 1957, General Electric Corporation introduced the Weathertron heat pump, a reverse-cycle heating and cooling unit. It was the perfect remedy for our dilemma. The heating cycle met air force guidelines. When the indoor temperature got too warm, the device automatically began pumping cool air inside and expelling the heat to the exterior. Colonel Twitty and I flew to Washington in his private military plane to propose using the new appliance. Recognizing the technology as a model solution, air force officials agreed to install Weathertron heat pumps in all of the Homestead AFB homes. Once the houses were occupied, the climate-control units met with such overwhelming approval that the air force revised its building regulations, enabling air-conditioning to be installed in other Capehart-era homes.

While I was working on the plans for Homestead in 1956, the air force asked me to design a residential community at Patrick Air Force Base in Cape Canaveral. This project established 999 units for the families of military personnel and civilian technicians working at the Air Force Missile Test Center and National Aeronautics and Space Administration (NASA). The design of the houses, landscaping, and streets was very similar to those in Homestead. In an effort to prevent monotony, I organized the neighborhoods so that there were no homes adjacent to or across the street from one another that were the same color or had the same front elevation.

The Air Force Space Command at Patrick AFB was respon-sible for providing launch support services for missiles, satellites, and, ultimately, manned space flights. One night while I was visiting the quarters of Major General D. N. Yates, the commanding officer of the facility, he turned to me and said, "Norman, if you look out of the window you will probably see something you are going to remember." Shortly thereafter, a rocket was launched. It was a magnificent sight and made me proud of the small part that I was contributing to the United States space program.

General D. N. Yates presenting the key to Master Sergeant George H. James and his family, the occupants of the first completed Capehart house at Patrick AFB, Cape Canaveral, Florida, 1958. I appear second from the left, wearing a fedora. Official Air Force photograph.

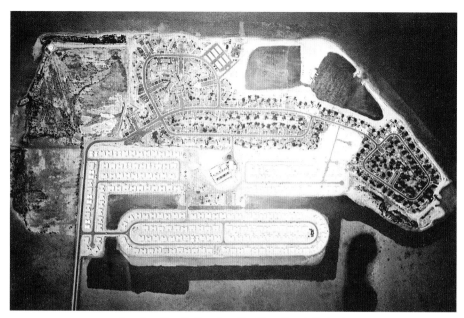

Capehart Family Housing, Key West Naval Air Station, Key West, 1960–62. The dark area at the bottom of this aerial photograph indicates where the sea floor was dredged. The new residential island is in its center.

Part of my commission for the Key West Naval Air Station residential development included actually creating the land on which the community would be built. Since space for five hundred more houses simply did not exist on the small island, my team of architects, engineers, and contractors had to create the site by dredging a portion of the Gulf of Mexico. Ultimately, over 1.8 million cubic yards of fill was removed from the sea floor in order to transform the shallow, underwater shore area adjacent to the base into dry land.

The high mineral content of Key West's soil had always made building in the city challenging. Even cast iron would deteriorate after a few years. Once the fill that my team excavated was tested, I learned that this ocean-bed soil was even more corrosive than normal, making it particularly difficult to select an appropriate material for the underground plumbing system. Once I began investigating nonmetal alternatives, I quickly found myself drawn to polyvinyl chloride (PVC) piping. PVC piping was light, durable, inexpensive, and noncorrosive. The rigid plastic tubing first appeared on the market in 1952. By the late 1950s, cast iron was still the material specified in most municipal building codes and favored by construction unions. Consequently, PVC piping had yet to be widely used for water and sewer systems. I could find only one company that produced the material, and then I had to have them teach all of the plumbers how to handle and install the plastic plumbing system. The efficiency of the resulting system, however, made the extra effort worth it. The extent to which I used PVC at the naval base garnered national attention. In 1961 I presented a case history of the project to the Building Research Institute of the American Academy of Sciences in Washington, D.C. The adoption of the new product by the U.S. Navy undoubtedly gave it a legitimacy that encouraged building code changes across the country.

With the residential communities of Homestead AFB, Patrick AFB, and the Key West Naval Air Station, I sought to provide better living conditions for military families stationed in Florida. The responsibility of planning the overall site design—the homes, the landscaping, and the infrastructure—gave me the chance to contribute more fully to how people lived their lives and defended the nation. The "contemporary" style homes and incorporation of innovative technologies, like the Weathertron heat pump and PVC piping, helped create a comfortable, modern environment that expressed the dynamic program of the U.S. military.

HEADQUARTERS
AIR FORCE MISSILE TEST CENTER
AIR RESEARCH AND DEVELOPMENT COMMAND
UNITED STATES AIR FORCE
Patrick Air Force Base, Florida

In reply address communication to Comdr,
AFMTC, attention following office symbol

MTF

FEB 10 1959

Norman N. Giller & Associates
975 Arthur Godfrey Road
Miami Beach, Florida

Gentlemen:

It is a pleasure to inform you that we have had many fine compliments on the 999 unit Capehart Housing Project constructed at this Base.

During the past month, Mr. Dewey Short, Assistant Secretary of the Army, visited the project and made very favorable comments as to construction, equipment and appearance. He said that he had not seen better Capehart Houses anywhere.

Also during January of this year, Mr. Neal Garlock, Assistant Secretary of the Air Force visited the Capehart Housing Project and was very much impressed with the houses. He especially commended the excellent planning, the quality construction and the overall attractive appearance of the finished area.

The project is an excellent example of the superior engineering and architectural capabilities of you and your organization.

I wish to again express my thanks and appreciation for your full cooperation in the completion of this project.

Sincerely,

D. N. YATES
Major General, USAF
Commander

In 1959, the Department of Defense determined that the community I designed for the Homestead AFB was the "Best Overall Designed Housing Project in All of the Military." The commanding officer of the base, Colonel Harold J. Whiteman, is presenting me with an award commemorating this honor (*left*). A letter I received from General Yates in 1959 regarding the homes at Patrick AFB (*right*). When Hurricane Andrew struck Homestead in 1992, the category-five storm destroyed beyond repair a significant portion of the base's residences. In 2002, Miami-Dade County converted the area into the Homestead Air Reserve Base Park.

SUPERMARKETS AND SHOPPING CENTERS

Just as suburban housing developments changed the way postwar Americans lived, supermarkets changed the way they shopped. Although the term *supermarket* first came into use in the 1930s, it was not until the 1950s that these large, self-service combination food stores became a part of American culture.[1] As incomes of families increased, the amount of money they were willing to spend on food rose as well. Concurrently, developments in food science and marketing strategies led to an explosion in the number of packaged food products. With dozens of types of frozen foods, prepared snacks, and boxed mixes becoming available each week, regional grocery store chains were forced to expand and consolidate their retail spaces in order to meet the demand and remain profitable.[2] Since automobiles were the major mode of transportation in suburban areas, markets no longer needed to be within walking distance of their customers. As food and dry goods stores across the country grew from four thousand square feet to ten thousand square feet and diversified their inventory, a "supermarket boom" was born. With their long aisles and overflowing shelves, supermarkets provided the hungry 1950s consumer with a previously unimaginable selection of grocery products.

Reflecting the supermarket trend, Philadelphia businessman Sam Friedland hired me in 1954 to plan a series of Food Fair supermarkets that would be larger than any other grocery stores in Florida at the time. Since the name *Food Fair* suggested to

Food Fair Supermarket, St. Petersburg, Florida, 1955. Photograph, 1958.

the average housewife that purchasing groceries did not have to be another form of domestic drudgery, shopping at these stores was an "experience." Consequently, my design choices worked to ensure that customers felt as if they were involved with the movement and excitement of the store.

In the 1940s and early 1950s, the exteriors of supermarkets were treated simply. The front façades of the rectangular structures featured large horizontal windows and overhanging entrance canopies. "Architectural theatrics" were not necessary as the mere opening of a large, modern food store was an exciting community event.[3] By 1954, however, supermarkets were beginning to become common. In an effort to attract customers and differentiate Food Fair from its competitors, I crowned the front of some of its supermarkets with a thirty-foot concrete arch. The entrance overhang that the arch supported projected fifteen feet beyond the building's plate-glass front walls. I placed the name of the store at the arch's apex so that the sign could be seen from a great distance. The enormous feature added pizzazz to the buildings and gave the chain a distinctive trademark.

By design, Food Fair's supermarket interiors gave the impression that there was always a lot of activity going on—activity that shoppers wanted to be a part of. Walls were bright and colorful. Ceilings and floors were made of hard materials in order to reflect the voices of customers and the ringing of cash registers. The layout followed standard practices: an abundant produce display was followed by rows of dry goods; a meat

Food Fair Properties Shopping Center, St. Petersburg, Florida, 1955. Rendering. By the time this shopping center was built, supermarkets had become an American institution, included on tours of the country by foreign dignitaries like Queen Elizabeth and Nikita Khrushchev.

FOOD FAIR SHOPPING CENTER
ST. PETERSBURG · FLORIDA
norman m.giller & associates
ARCHITECTS

department was located at the back of the store; and small impulse items lined checkout counters. The buildings' simple rectangular shapes best accommodated the long aisles that spilled over with TV dinners, frozen fish sticks, instant puddings, and Rice-A-Roni, new, easy-to-prepare food products whose vibrant packaging competed for the housewife's eye and space in her shopping cart.

A large parking lot was another supermarket design essential. Ample parking added to the convenience of supermarket-style shopping and reflected the preferences of an increasingly mobile suburban population. Roomy midcentury cars enabled consumers to bring large quantities of items home quickly and easily. By the mid-1950s, supermarket properties provided more space for cars than they did for people.

Food Fair Properties Shopping Center, West Palm Beach, Florida, 1958. Rendering. There is a playfulness to the architectural elements along the open-air corridor of this strip shopping center. The heavy concrete overhang appears to be supported by the thin, plate-glass display windows, on the left, and the exposed steel buttresses, on the right. Together with the planters, these airy details create a transition from outdoor area to enclosed retail space.

After 1955, freestanding Food Fair supermarket buildings began to be incorporated into multi-unit shopping-center strips. This building type was essentially a variation of the Main Street model modified for increased automobile traffic. The basic concept—a unified row of stores set back from the road by a front parking area—first appeared in outlying urban areas as early as 1907. Their numbers slowly increased in the 1920s and 1930s. With the postwar expansion of suburbia, the neighborhood shopping center became widespread.[4]

As the Florida market continued to grow in the 1950s, Food Fair Properties began developing their own commercial centers, over twenty of which I planned. Typically, a Food Fair

supermarket would anchor one end of the property and a national chain store like Woolworth's or W. T. Grant's would anchor the other end. The smaller commercial spaces in between would be rented by local, independent businesses, which benefited from the traffic created by the larger stores. A spacious parking lot completed the design.

The convenience provided by strip shopping centers made them popular alternatives to shopping in downtown areas. By the 1960s, they seemed to be on every suburban corner. During a speech about the design and proliferation of the building type I gave at the 1962 International Council of Shopping Centers Convention, I could not help but remark that one of the audience members was destined to open a shopping center in outer space.

Food Fair Properties Shopping Center, South Florida, ca. 1957. Crowds of shoppers overflow into the parking lot while waiting to experience Woolworth's Grand Opening Celebration.

THE GILLER BUILDING

The Giller Building sits at the gateway to Miami Beach, greeting visitors and residents as they cross Biscayne Bay from mainland Miami on the Julia Tuttle Causeway. While its glass-tiled, multi-colored tower has become a Miami Beach landmark, the Giller Building had much more humble beginnings.

By 1955, Miami had grown tremendously, and the architecture firm of norman m. giller & associates had grown with it. For many years, the firm was located in the penthouse office of the Mercantile Bank Building on Lincoln Road and Washington Avenue. The view of the Atlantic Ocean and the heart of Miami Beach was quite remarkable. When one of the bank officers discovered it, he convinced the chairman to turn the penthouse into an officers' lounge rather than renew the Giller office lease. Instead of finding another space to rent, I decided it was time to house the firm in its own office building.

The nature of architectural firms is that they regularly grow and shrink in size based on the work available. I needed a space flexible enough to house my fifty employees but also capable of being left unused without costing the business much money when I accepted fewer commissions. At the time, commercial development on Miami Beach had begun moving northward from the Lincoln Road area. Arthur Godfrey Road/Forty-first Street had successfully emerged as a commercial area. I found myself interested in the property at its sleepy western end

where the street terminated at Alton Road. In those days, the land was very inexpensive, and I ultimately purchased two lots.

I initially envisioned the Giller Building as a two-story general office building. My intention was to put the firm on the first floor and rent out the second floor in order to pay the mortgage. By the time the plans were complete, however, I had leased the entire second story. Once I decided to build a third floor, the same thing happened. By the time those plans were complete, the additional spaces also had been leased. At that

Giller Building, Miami Beach, 1955–61. Advertisement, late 1950s. Since there was limited office space on Miami Beach at the time, advertisements for the Giller Building generated much community interest.

Giller Building, Miami Beach, 1955–61. Photograph, 2001.

point, I resolved to add a fourth story, which my firm would occupy, and make the first floor into additional rental space. The city was growing so rapidly and the demand for office space was so great that when the building opened in 1957, all of the offices were full.

The design of the Giller Building blends utility with my ongoing interest in color, texture, and unusual details. In order to accommodate the slightly curved southern and western property lines, the structure's southern wall runs along the street at a diagonal. Consequently, the southwest and southeast corners of the building meet at obtuse and acute angles, respectively, rather than standard right angles. These atypical corners endow the primary elevation with an unexpected angularity.

The building's most distinctive element is its colorful rectangular tower. A geometrically patterned red, green, and yellow glass-tile mosaic decorates its façade. The glass shimmers in the

Giller Building, Miami Beach, 1955–61. Photograph, 1956. Family members and employees of norman m. giller & associates at the groundbreaking for the Giller Building.

The drafting room of norman giller & associates, Mercantile Bank Building, Miami Beach, ca. 1955 (*above*), Giller Building, Miami Beach, 1955–61. The firm's new drafting room, at full capacity in 1958 (*below*).

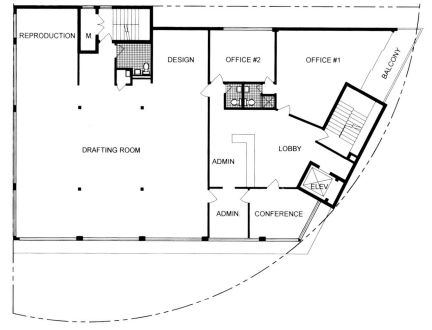

Giller Building, Miami Beach, 1955–61. Fourth-floor plan showing the curved southern and western property lines and the building's angled front elevation.

Giller Building, Miami Beach, 1955–61. Photograph, 1963.

Florida sunshine, adding color and texture to a large section of the front of the structure. Since the rain keeps the glass tiles clean, they also serve as a relatively maintenance-free embellishment. Both the exterior and interior of this tower emphasize the building's vertical mass. The façade's tiled mosaic guides the viewer's eye skyward. Inside, an elevator and stairway climb the tower's five stories to the roof.

The Giller Building's glass entrance is underneath the tall tiled block. A distinctive, hanging stairway is visible through the glass wall; when viewed from the outside, its apparent weightlessness contrasts with the heavy tiled surface. I made the stair structure appear to float in order to encourage its users to stop for a moment and study its mechanics. Thin, steel, aluminum-encased rods hang from the ceiling, supporting the terrazzo stairs. Seen from a distance, the stairway seems to rise mysteriously and disappear behind the massive tiled wall.

A band of ribbon windows protected by thin cantilevered overhangs interrupts the otherwise solid western, northern, and eastern façades. The horizontal orientation of these elements balances the tiled tower and indicates the division of floors. The position of the windows allows light to filter into the offices while freeing wall space for tenants to use as they see fit. The landscaping scheme features tropical plants and sabal palm trees.

The balconies and full-length windows at the building's southeast corner also offset the heaviness of the mosaic panel and provide depth to the façade. The offices with balconies are rented as premium spaces. I initially placed some of my firm's renderings and models in a small room behind the plate-glass

Giller Building, Miami Beach, 1955–61. Photograph, 2003. The firm, renamed Giller & Giller, Inc., still occupies the fourth floor.

first-floor walls. After discovering that the sun's heat would damage anything left in there, I was forced to merge this space with the adjoining area.

My private office has always occupied the fourth floor's southeast corner. The office's ten-foot entrance door runs the entire height of the wall. The brass doorknob, which is decorated with a starburst door plate, is four feet above the floor. Due to the diagonal front façade, the room gradually narrows as one walks into it. Since a garden-variety rectangular desk would not have fit the space, I designed a desk circular in one section and long and curvy in the other. The round section sits in the wider part of the room and is used to host meetings for up to six people. The longer, thinner section extends into the narrower area and can comfortably seat seven people. The placement of the aluminum ceiling lights echoes the unusual form of the desk. My chair is at the point where the two sections connect. The entire desk is made of Formica with a faux wood-grain finish. It was a good choice of materials—after forty-seven years of use, the desk is still in terrific condition.

When state and federal officials built a new causeway that connected mainland Miami to Miami Beach at the western end

Norman M. Giller's private office, Giller Building, Miami Beach, 1955–61. A map of the United States adorns the wood-paneled walls behind my desk. There is a secret button on the floor by my chair. When pressed, the section of the panel behind the map slides open, and a spotlight switches on. At the most opportune moment during a meeting with a client, I would push the button, revealing an illuminated drawing of my proposed design. This theatrical gesture won them over every time.

of Arthur Godfrey Road in 1961, the Giller Building unexpectedly found itself in the spotlight. Thanks to the busy Julia Tuttle Causeway, the quiet end of the street became a hub of activity.

In the months following the causeway's opening, I received so many inquiries regarding available office space that I decided to design and build a six-story addition on the northeast side of the property. It was important, however, that the new wing span the parking lot, as free parking had become a draw for our tenants. When the addition was completed, the first mayor of Miami-Dade County, Chuck Hall, and his wife, Jackie, lived on the sixth floor and worked out of their travel agency on the fifth floor. Their apartment included an indoor swimming pool formed from one-inch steel plates, rather than heavier concrete slabs. The pool was enclosed by sliding glass doors and a retractable roof. The unobstructed view from the apartment was spectacular. The Halls lived in the Giller Building until the mid-1980s. I later had the pool removed and converted the area into office space.

The Giller Building represents a milestone in my professional career. Upon completion of the first wing in 1957, the structure was believed to be the largest office building in the South owned, occupied, and designed by an architect. The relocation and expansion of my firm's headquarters was well-timed. The number of commissions I received that year was so large that norman m. giller & associates earned a place in *Architectural Forum*'s listing of the biggest architectural firms in the country, by construction volume.

Listing from *Architectural Forum*, September 1958.

One hundred offices handle almost 10 per cent of all the building design in the U. S.

Architecture's biggest firms

	Firm	1957 ($000)	1958 (est.) ($000)	Industrial	Office	School	Hospital & Institution	Other	Employees
		Construction put in place		Type of construction put in place as a per cent of 1957 volume					
1	Giffels & Rossetti (Detroit)	250,000	190,000	60	10	9	6	15	850
2	Skidmore, Owings & Merrill (New York)	150,700	74,200	6	30	19	7	38	1066
3	Daniel, Mann, Johnson & Mendenhall (Los Angeles)	150,000	200,000	10	23	20	7	40	480
4	Eggers & Higgins (New York)	130,000	130,000	2	30	30	28	10	245
5	Erwin Gerber & A. Pancani Jr. (Newark)	110,000	150,000	8	3	0	11	78	78
6	Emery Roth & Sons (New York)	110,000	135,000	0	90	7.5	0	2.5	58
7	Albert Kahn Assoc. Archts. & Engrs., Inc. (Detroit)	108,000	N.A.	78	19	1.5	1.5	0	290
8	Welton Becket & Assocs. (Los Angeles)	104,750	130,000	8	36	12	24	20	427
9	Perkins & Will (Chicago)	102,582	158,000	1	15	83	0	1	187
10	Norman M. Giller & Assocs. (Miami Beach)	101,000	60,000	5	10	5	2	78	62
11	Leo A. Daly Co. (Omaha)	100,000	130,000	10	15	20	10	45	250
12	George M. Ewing Co. (Philadelphia)	99,500	70,000	39	2	24	19	16	200
13	Harrison & Abramovitz (New York)	98,000	125,000	0	60	11	17.5	11.5	160
14	A. Epstein & Sons, Inc. (Chicago)	80,000	80,000	40	23	2	7	28	150
15	Kahn & Jacobs (New York)	80,000	70,000	15	60	10	10	5	98
16	Voorhees, Walker, Smith & Smith (New York)	77,099	90,000	3	45	5	15	32	550
17	Smith, Hinchman & Grylls Assocs., Inc. (Detroit)	74,934	80,000	10	5	5	70	10	287
18	Kelly & Gruzen (New York)	70,000	N.A.	1	1	40	5	53	95
19	J. E. Stanton & William F. Stockwell (Los Angeles)	70,000	30,000	0	15	30	0	55	95
20	S. J. Kessler & Sons (New York)	60,000	60,000	10	5	15	0	70	42
21	J. E. Sirrine Co. (Greenville, S.C.)	60,000	40,000	95	0.4	3	0.8	0.8	250
22	A. M. Kinney Assocs. & affiliates (Cincinnati)	59,500	80,000	32	6	6	4	52	235
23	Adrian Wilson & Assocs. (Los Angeles)	58,000	45,000	15	15	10	15	45	195
24	Arthur Froehlich & Assocs. (Beverly Hills)	54,600	25,000	0	0.8	0.8	0	98.4	65
25	H. A. Kuljian & Co. (Philadelphia)	52,100	45,000	67	6	8	8	11	160
26	Reynolds, Smith & Hills (Jacksonville)	50,216	35,000	14	0	5	24	57	195
27	Victor Gruen Assocs. (Los Angeles)	50,000	70,000	10	20	5	5	60	150
28	John C. Lindsay & Assocs. (Santa Monica)	50,000	50,000	20	25	20	5	30	41
29	Schmidt, Garden & Erikson (Chicago)	49,000	45,000	20	0	10	70	0	137
30	Hudgins, Thompson, Ball & Assocs. (Oklahoma City)	47,500	50,000	24	8	25	6	37	197
31	Hayes, Seay, Mattern & Mattern (Roanoke)	46,000	50,000	10	4	19	37	30	130
32	Albert C. Martin & Assocs. (Los Angeles)	45,737	35,000	15	5	10	20	50	264
33	Harley, Ellington & Day, Inc. (Detroit)	45,000	60,000	30	5	20	10	35	183
34	Sargent, Webster, Crenshaw & Folley (Syracuse)	45,000	45,000	8	7	70	5	10	181
35	Frank Grad & Sons (Newark)	41,760	45,295	20	24	4	2	50	111
36	Holabird & Root & Burgee (Chicago)	40,000	49,500	26	20	20	5	29	290
37	Naramore, Bain, Brady & Johanson (Seattle)	40,000	40,000	30	0	25	25	20	200
38	Frederic P. Wiedersum Assocs. (Valley Stream, N.Y.)	39,299	45,000	0	1	97	1	1	138
39	Toltz, King, Duvall, Anderson & Assocs., Inc. (St. Paul)	38,000	38,000	24	0	23	30	23	101
40	Ellerbe & Co. (St. Paul)	35,000	35,000	20	15	20	30	15	290
41	Robert & Co. Assocs. (Atlanta)	35,000	40,000	15	30	13	6	36	235
42	John S. Bolles (San Francisco)	32,500	21,000	72	9	6	1	12	40
43	Lublin, McGaughy & Assocs. (Norfolk)	32,500	40,000	3.1	4.6	30.8	6.1	55.4	208
44	Six Assocs., Inc. (Asheville, N.C.)	32,350	N.A.	12	4	14	10	60	62
45	Naess & Murphy (Chicago)	32,000	35,000	13	54	17	0	16	143
46	J. N. Pease & Co. (Charlotte)	32,000	40,000	15	10	5	10	60	110
47	Pace Assocs. (Chicago)	31,530	50,800	19.4	5.9	3.9	59.4	11.4	150
48	Gehron & Seltzer (New York)	30,000	28,000	0	0	63	29	8	50
49	Vincent G. Kling (Philadelphia)	30,000	39,000	10	30	25	20	15	85
50	Meriwether, Marye & Assocs. (Lexington, Ky.)	30,000	30,000	0	0	25	65	10	31

NOTES: This list does not include so-called package-building firms, which combine design with construction. N.A. means data not available. "Other" includes housing, hotels, churches, stores, banks, research laboratories, public buildings, recreational facilities, garages, and civil engineering projects.

SINGAPORE HOTEL

Although I had always enjoyed the challenges that came with designing different building types, by the mid-1950s I had become somewhat of a motel specialist. The interest generated by this achievement encouraged me to experiment with more innovative architectural forms.

In 1956, I proposed a fifteen-story cylindrical hotel design to developers William Praver and Melvin G. Rubel for their Rubiyat Hotel. The pie-shaped guest rooms gradually widened from the entrance door toward the exterior wall. Elevator shafts, stairwells, and electrical, air-conditioning, and plumbing systems were placed in the cylinder's central core. This clustering of the building's mechanical elements made the structure very efficient. Access to guest rooms was via a circular hallway that wrapped around the core. The smaller hallway allowed the rooms to be a bit larger than average.

Influenced by Motel Row marketing strategies, I believed the structure's departure from straight lines and cubical spaces would help attract guests. To my knowledge, the Rubiyat Hotel would have been the first cylindrical hotel. Yet, I soon discovered that no matter how architecturally innovative a design may be, if the developers are unable to secure funding, the project will never be realized.

Mr. Praver and Mr. Rubel believed my distinctive plan for the large Bal Harbour resort would effectively combine the luxury

Singapore Hotel, Bal Harbour, Florida, 1957 (demolished). Postcard.

of the hotels in Miami Beach, immediately to the south, with the informality of the motels in Sunny Isles, immediately to the north. The bankers that they approached were not convinced, however, that the proposal would translate into a profitable hotel operation. The three twentieth-century buildings most celebrated for their circular shape—the Capitol Records Tower in Los Angeles (Welton Becket and Associates, 1956), Solomon R. Guggenheim Museum in New York (Frank Lloyd Wright, 1956–59), and Marina City in Chicago (Bertram Goldberg, 1964)—had yet to prove the commercial success of the format.

Since the bankers did not have enough vision to take the risk, I was forced to redesign the hotel using the pedestal-and-tower formula typical of midcentury Miami Beach resort complexes.[1] A seven-story tower of guest rooms ran along the site's northern boundary. As with the Thunderbird Motel, I reserved the tower's west-facing wall for signage. Long, uninterrupted concrete balconies decorated the northern and southern sides of the tower. A large lobby featuring curtain walls of glass and a ranch-style roof ran the full length of the property's western boundary.

Behind the lobby was a spacious pool and outdoor recreation area. In addition to relaxing by the pools or on the beach, guests could play mini-golf, table tennis, or shuffleboard. The resort organized beach barbecues and weekly plays. Throughout the day, children had access to their own playroom, and adults could peruse the arcade of shops or have

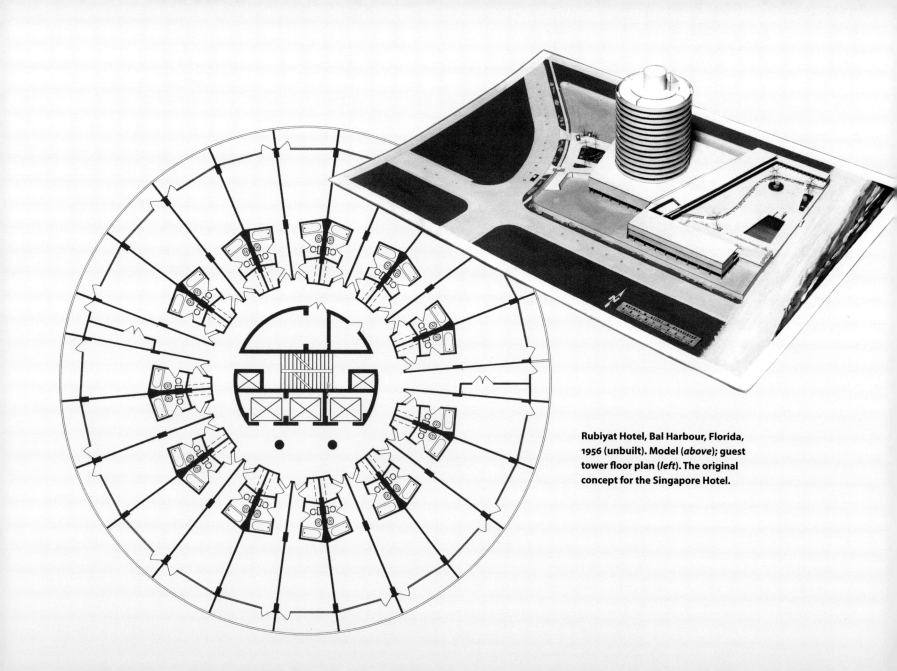

Rubiyat Hotel, Bal Harbour, Florida, 1956 (unbuilt). Model (*above*); guest tower floor plan (*left*). The original concept for the Singapore Hotel.

Singapore Hotel, Bal Harbour, Florida, 1957 (demolished). Promotional brochure.

the SINGAPORE enchantingly different...
romantically gay

lunch at the informal restaurant. At night, dinner was offered in the posh dining room, and guests were entertained by shows at the hotel's elegant nightclub. I designed a special nightclub for teenagers as well. Each guest room featured a 21-inch television set, still a huge draw for travelers. The success of the 240-room hotel, renamed the Singapore, as well as neighboring resorts like the Americana (Morris Lapidus, 1956), exemplified the public's growing desire for casually chic Florida vacation opportunities.

EXECUTIVE MOTOR HOTEL

As Motel Row's fame and success grew, entrepreneurs from around the country approached me to design tourist accommodations that would bring modern, affordable MiMo glamour to their own regions. Virginia businessman Henry Stern came across my motels while on vacation in Key West and Sunny Isles. In 1958, he commissioned me to design a motel in Richmond that would also function as an efficient headquarters for small conventions and meetings. At the time, Richmond's architecture was dominated by heavy, traditional brick build-

ings. Mr. Stern wanted his motor hotel to be one of the first "contemporary" structures built in the city. Producing a light, lively building that would catch the eye of speeding motorists was essential.

Richmond's virtually hurricane-free summers allowed me to incorporate larger expanses of glass into my design than was possible in South Florida. I placed a double-height lobby entirely enclosed in glass along the front of the property. During the day, the 25-foot glass panels would seem shockingly

Executive Motor Hotel, Richmond, Virginia, 1958. Postcard.

Aristocrat Motel, Hot Springs, Arkansas, 1960. Rendering (*above left*). Hobbs Hotel and Regional Convention Center, Hobbs, New Mexico, 1962. Rendering (*above right*). Sahara Motel, Cleveland, Ohio, 1958 (*left*). Henry Stern was one of a number of out-of-state entrepreneurs who came to me eager to repeat the success of the Sunny Isles resort motel type. Here are three examples of other commissions I received for "contemporary" motor hotels across the country.

transparent. At night, the entire pavilion would seem to glow. To create a sense of rhythm and movement, I angled the walls rather than placing them square. The use of glass curtain walls, however, was so new to Richmond that Mr. Stern initially had difficulty finding a contractor in the area who knew how to properly install them.

Reinforcing the feeling of motion and playfulness, I repeated the zigzag pattern of the glass walls in the concrete porte cochere. A three-story-tall, curved rear wall anchors the sleek glass lobby. Decorated with the same glass mosaic tiles I used in the Giller Building, the deep-turquoise color and glimmering texture contrast with the smooth transparency of the glass. The curved, paneled wall extends through the length of the lobby and up beyond the ceiling. Inside, the concave exterior wall gives way to an S-shaped interior one. A grand cantilevered staircase nimbly climbs the wall's curvilinear surface, leading guests to the second-floor meeting and banquet rooms. Underneath the stairway, a long, tiled fountain accords the space an air of luxury. Imposing chandeliers and Mies van der Rohe–style furnishings complete the look.

"The Miami Beach Modern motel on a bleak stretch of highway in southern Delaware reminds the jaded driver of the welcome luxury of a tropical resort."
—Robert Venturi, Denise Scott Brown, and Steven Izenour, *Learning from Las Vegas*, 1972.

Executive Motor Hotel, Richmond, Virginia, 1958. The glass-enclosed lobby at night (*left*); dining room, with a view into the lobby area (*right*). In 1999, the Executive Motor Hotel, renamed the Inns of Virginia, was featured in the movie *Forces of Nature*, starring Sandra Bullock and Ben Affleck. Although the glimmering turquoise tile wall has since been painted beige, the zigzag glass curtain wall remains.

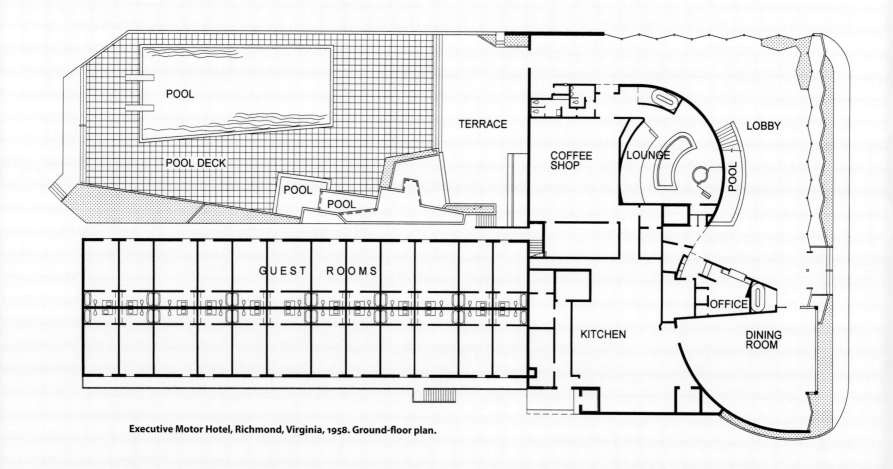

POOL

POOL DECK

POOL

POOL

TERRACE

COFFEE
SHOP

LOUNGE

LOBBY

POOL

GUEST   ROOMS

KITCHEN

OFFICE

DINING
ROOM

Executive Motor Hotel, Richmond, Virginia, 1958. Ground-floor plan.

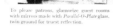
Advertisement for Parallel-O-Plate glass featuring the Executive Motor Hotel, 1962.

The motor hotel's 140 guest rooms are located in a long, low building behind the lobby. The layout of the rooms is based on the formula I had developed at the Ocean Palm. The three floors of back-to-back rooms are accessed via private entrances along covered, column-free catwalks. Adjacent to the guest room wing is a pool and patio area. The pool has speakers, so guests can listen to music while underwater, and lights, so that they can swim at night.

According to a promotional brochure, the motor hotel combined "strategically located luxury" (minutes from downtown Richmond) with "space-age" meeting facilities (closed-circuit television system, sound-proofed, climate-controlled rooms) in order to effectively unite business and pleasure. In a city of brick buildings, the Executive Motor Hotel announced the arrival of a modern age. Staying at the motel was "An Adventure in Itself!"

CARILLON HOTEL

The Carillon Hotel commission that I received from Al Kaskell in 1957 demanded creativity, skillful engineering, and business acumen. Before he had even hired an architect, Al determined that his building would be named 1958's "Hotel of the Year." During each season of the 1950s hotel boom, the newest hotel also became the most sought after. For Al, completing a spectacular luxury hotel in time for the busy Christmas tourist season was of utmost importance.

The Carillon Hotel sits on a four-acre oceanfront lot in the North Beach section of Miami Beach. As had become standard, I organized the property into three areas: a multistory guest-room building, a low central structure housing an expansive lobby and public facilities, and a beachfront pool area and cabana club. At the time, I was working with a structural engineer who had become familiar with a new building technique, flat-slab construction. Conventionally, construction of multi-story buildings utilized twelve inches of support consisting of a four-inch concrete slab plus an eight-inch concrete beam. At that depth, every floor added an additional foot to the overall height of the building. With flat-slab construction, however, a single six-inch concrete slab replaced the twelve-inch beam-and-slab combination. In the 1950s, the City of Miami Beach limited building heights to 150 feet above grade, which meant that the tower could only be fourteen stories tall. Flat-slab construction, however, enabled me to add an entire floor of forty

Carillon Hotel, Miami Beach, 1957–58 (altered). Rendering.

guest rooms without exceeding the height restriction. The resourceful plan translated into additional revenue for the owner of the hotel, my client. Not surprisingly, when I introduced this idea to Al, he was very pleased.

Providing benefits above and beyond what the client expects is an important gauge of a successful design. Here, using an innovative system created a better structure and a happier client. I believe the Carillon was the first high-rise structure

Carillon Hotel, Miami Beach, 1957–58 (altered). North elevation. True to modernist form, I used the structural grid pattern as a decorative element. The horizontal lines, for instance, are the six-inch concrete slabs that support each floor. I used aluminum window frames to create a secondary grid, reinforcing the rhythm of the first.

built in the South using flat-slab construction. The technique was a tremendous step forward. Today, flat-slab construction is widely used to build skyscrapers in Florida and elsewhere.

By the time the Carillon's design concept had been resolved, it was already February 1958. With the height restriction working to my benefit, I could fully concentrate on the feat of completing a sixteen-story hotel and resort complex in nine months! In order to do this, I fast-tracked the construction process. Working drawings were made in order to determine the total load that each of the facility's columns could carry. After the load factor was established, I was able to create the foundation plan. While the subcontractors and their suppli-

ers prepared their materials and delivered them to the site, my staff and I were designing the rest of the building. Once the structural components were on paper and given to the general contractors, my employees developed specs for the electrical, ventilation, and plumbing systems. As each segment was completed, it was given to the contractors to build. The architectural drawings always had to be one step ahead of the construction. Getting all of them made on time turned out to be a tremendous job, much larger than with the Copa City, which I had fast-tracked ten years earlier. The details involved in designing a sixteen-story upscale hotel required over one hundred hand-drawn sheets.

Carillon Hotel, Miami Beach, 1957–58 (altered). Accordion-fold concrete canopy plan.

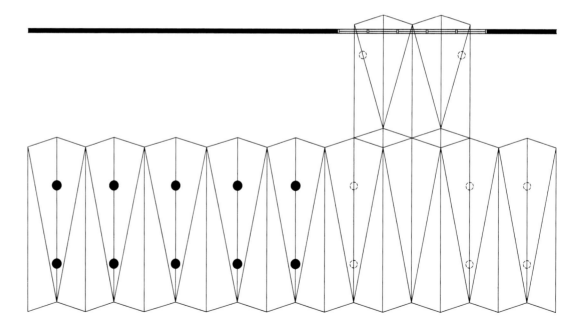

Carillon Hotel, Miami Beach, 1957–58 (altered). Two views of the hotel in the late 1990s: the circular pattern at the top of the tower originally designed to hold a row of giant bells (*above*); the accordion-fold canopy above the driveway sheltering guests and their cars from the elements (*right*). Between 2004 and 2007, the Carillon Hotel was remodeled by the architecture firm Arquitectonica and is now part of Canyon Ranch Living–Miami Beach, a condominium and hotel complex.

The hotel's name, as well as one of its most distinguishing architectural features, was inspired by Al's daughter, Carol. A carillon is a musical instrument composed of a row of bells arranged in chromatic sequence. When the bells are sounded together, a concordant harmony is produced. The row of large, open circles along the top of the tower was intended to hold oversized bells to be rung throughout the day, in honor of Carol Kaskell.

While the carillon was never actually installed, the sound and movement of ringing bells informed the hotel's lively ornamen-tation scheme. The zigzag concrete canopy above the main entrance resembles the folds of an accordion. Like a carillon, an accordion generates sound through the back-and-forth motion of its parts. I repeated the accordion-fold pattern vertically on the façade of the southern wing. The unexpected detail created a striking, three-story feature along the 141-foot section facing Collins Avenue. The sun's movement throughout the day generated a continually changing pattern of shadows across this west-facing folded surface. The roof of the lobby also was painted with a two-dimensional version of this accordion-fold

Carillon Hotel, Miami Beach, 1957–58 (altered). View of the guest tower, as seen from the pool area. Since the façade's glass walls were not load-bearing, I was free to place them wherever I liked. Recessing the wall created a balcony space, while placing it flush enabled sun to directly stream into the room for a longer period of time. By alternating recessed and flush sections, I was able to create a simple pattern.

"It's incredible that so much can be under one roof."
—*Miami Beach Sun*, October 1958.

pattern. Normally these sections were unadorned, flat, square areas. I wanted guests to easily recognize the repetition of elements when they looked out of their hotel room windows.

The Carillon opened on schedule and to much fanfare in October 1958. As Al had intended, the resort was quickly recognized as the "Hotel of the Year." With 620 guest rooms, the Carillon was, for a time, the largest hotel in Miami Beach. In addition to these accommodations, the facility also included an enormous convention center, a nightclub, a formal dining room and an informal coffee shop, a large pool area, solariums, an arcade of shops, and a large parking garage—all of the features, amenities, and conveniences convention seekers could hope to find in one luxury location. Virtually a self-contained city, the Carillon attracted the type of guest who wanted the pleasantries only a top resort hotel could provide.

I remember being very amused by the comments made by the radio announcer during his live national broadcast from the hotel on opening day. Although the city was in the middle of an unseasonable cold snap, he kept urging listeners to escape the winter weather by taking a trip to tropical Miami Beach.

For a number of years the nightclub at the Carillon was run by Lou Walters, father of the television journalist Barbara Walters. His elaborate revues, featuring showgirls, singers, dancers, comedians, and musicians, helped make the Carillon one of the hottest spots on the North Beach strip.

Carillon Hotel, Miami Beach, 1957–58
(altered). The entrance to the Carillon's
grand lobby was accessed by a rather
dramatic ramp. When visitors got out
of their car, they were already one story
above ground. A stairwell in the central
part of the lobby connected it to the
shops at street level. I placed the large,
decorative aluminum screen (*above and
left*), around the stairway to help guide
visitors and guests.

DIPLOMAT HOTEL AND COUNTRY CLUB

The sophisticated, grand Diplomat Hotel and Country Club in Hollywood, Florida, was the most extraordinary project I designed during the postwar years. By the mid-1950s, Miami Beach had become America's entertainment capital. The Diplomat was designed to compete with the most glamorous resorts in Miami Beach, hotels like the Fontainebleau (Lapidus, 1953) and its progeny. In contrast to Lapidus's pastiche "Modern French Provincial" or "Contemporary Italian Renaissance," the Diplomat was pure "Ultra-Modern Luxury." It provided the rich and the famous who visited each season with the ultimate elegant vacation experience.

The Diplomat Hotel, the centerpiece of the resort, sat on one thousand feet of exclusive beachfront property and featured elegant guest rooms, chic nightclubs, swanky lounges, rambling pool areas, extensive recreational facilities, sumptuous dining salons, an opulent grand ballroom, and magnificent ocean views. An eighteen-hole championship golf course and additional party rooms, cocktail lounges, tennis courts, and card rooms could be found at the plush 150-acre Diplomat Country Club, a mile to the northwest. In addition to the thousands of guests who stayed at the Diplomat, the complex was host to extravagant birthday parties for Jackie Gleason and President Gerald Ford, Danny Thomas's celebrity golf tournament, Frank Sinatra's emergence-from-retirement party, Peter Lawford's emceeing of the John F. Kennedy Memorial Charity Ball, and concerts by Judy Garland, Diana Ross, Liza Minelli, Sammy Davis Jr., Tony Bennett, and Bob Hope.

When Sam Friedland came to me in 1956 to discuss the construction of a motel, there was no way to know that the resulting commission would become my masterpiece. Sam was a repeat client—since 1954, I had been designing his Food Fair supermarkets and shopping centers. During one of our first meetings for this project, we decided to drive north from my Miami Beach office to survey the property. Our route took us past Sunny Isles' Motel Row. As we drove by the Thunderbird Motel, Sam mentioned that he envisioned me designing the same type of facility on his land.

Diplomat Hotel and Country Club, Hollywood, Florida, 1956–58 (demolished). Hotel entrance (*left*); country club entrance (*right*). Over five hundred mature palm trees had to be planted before opening day.

As we approached the Hollywood plot, Route A1A narrowed considerably, with marshland and mangrove swamp where motels had risen farther south. Much of Friedland's land was under two feet of water. Instead of tourists, there were land crabs—thousands of them crawling in every direction. I could hear them crunch under the tires as we drove around the site.

Sam and I spent about six months discussing details of the commission before I put any ideas on paper. Our initial plan called for a 150-acre golf course and a four-story luxury motel. While I was working on the drawings and specifications, Sam decided that he wanted to build an upscale hotel, as well. After touring the grounds, the general manager he had hired to run the facility became convinced that the land was too large and too valuable to use for a mere motel. He believed that building a hotel on the property's beachfront section would prove to be a more worthwhile investment. By the time ground was broken in November 1956, the enterprise had evolved into three independent projects: the Diplomat Country Club (1956–57), the Envoy Motel (1957), and the Diplomat Hotel (1957–58).

The development and coordination of this venture were so elaborate that thirty-five of my employees, almost half the staff

Diplomat Country Club, Hollywood, Florida, 1956–57 (demolished). Clubhouse, exterior view (*top left*). The flatness of the landscape complemented the elongated design of the club building. Due to the large size of the property, there really was no need to build a multistory structure; Calcutta Room, interior view (*left*). I elevated the hall two feet above grade so diners could easily see the players on the expansive golf course designed by Robert Lawrence.

at the time, worked continuously for months on the Diplomat complex. The first major component of the job was to transform the mangroves and marshland into the golf course. In order to have enough fill to raise the land level by three feet, Sam had to purchase a square-mile property in the western part of Hollywood. For over a year, trucks transported dirt from the inland borrow site to the project area near the ocean. Ultimately, 1.6 million yards of fill were carried in over 320,000 trips.

After the site was filled and the golf course planned, the Diplomat Country Club's 600-foot long clubhouse was built. I used sleek, "contemporary" materials to give the structure the sheer, informal elegance a modernistic Florida clubhouse demanded. I enveloped the club's main dining and dancing hall, the Calcutta Room, in double-height glass walls to create the atmosphere of an open pavilion. The diamond-shaped steel panels attached to the exposed steel support columns added rhythm and pattern to the otherwise pared-down structure. Wood, copper, and stone, as well as earth-toned fabrics, added warmth to the décor. The glass walls made the room seem so airy that when the drapes were pulled back, it was almost like sitting outdoors. The cantilevered roof shaded and protected the interior spaces and exterior loggia. The building also housed men's and women's locker rooms and a pro shop that sold luxury sporting goods.

Envoy Motel (Diplomat West), Hollywood, Florida, 1957 (demolished). Broad, column-free walkways lined with offset aluminum railings overlooked the motel's grounds and parking area.

The Envoy Motel, later referred to as the Diplomat West, was the second component of the resort to be completed. The motel was built on the western side of a narrow strip of land between the Atlantic Ocean and the Intracoastal Waterway. The three-building facility included 150 guest rooms, an informal dining room, and a cocktail lounge. The entrance pavilion was enclosed in glass, like the Calcutta Room, and crowned with a thick concrete roof slab. Although the hefty roof appeared to be supported by the ethereal walls, it was actually bolstered by

Envoy Motel (Diplomat West), Hollywood, Florida, 1957 (demolished). The distinctive concrete *V* supports sat on an angle toward Route A1A. The detail was intended to attract passing motorists (*left*); guest room, interior view. A couple enjoying the motel's chic informality can be seen through the room's glass wall. Parking spaces adjacent to the lower level guest rooms provided added convenience (*above*).

a giant pair of wide, concrete, V-shaped piers that sat at either end of the pavilion. For added drama and whimsy, I rested a large, concrete balcony in the center of each of these piers. To passengers whizzing by on Route A1A, the heavy balconies seemed delicately balanced on the column's edges.

I modeled the two guest-room buildings on the designs I created for my earlier Motel Row clients: rooms arranged back to back and accessed by private entrances along a concrete, column-free catwalk. The outward-facing wall of each room was made of glass, enabling guests to enjoy views of the Intracoastal Waterway or the landscaped pool area. Some of the

units included kitchenettes for guests interested in extended stays. As an added amenity for families, I incorporated a kiddie pool, sandbox, and rec room. A long, curving, covered walkway, reminiscent of the free-form canopies of Oscar Niemeyer, connected the guest rooms to the large swimming pool and patio area. Beyond this, the motel's small marina on the Intracoastal Waterway offered a water shuttle that took guests to the Diplomat Country Club, located about a mile northwest. The Envoy's association with the fashionable luxury hotel and country club made it an especially appealing destination for middle-class guests eager to live out their leisure fantasies.

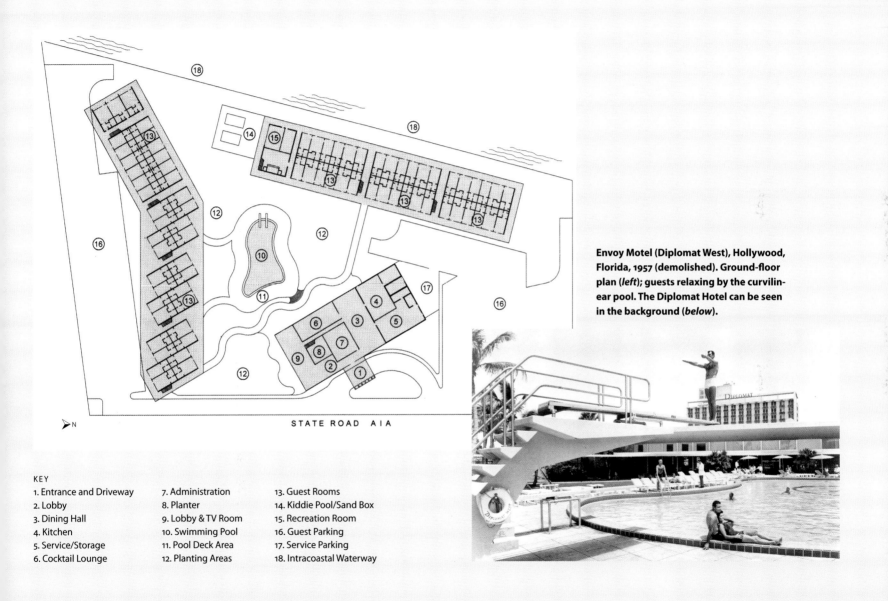

Envoy Motel (Diplomat West), Hollywood, Florida, 1957 (demolished). Ground-floor plan (*left*); guests relaxing by the curvilinear pool. The Diplomat Hotel can be seen in the background (*below*).

STATE ROAD A1A

➤N

KEY

1. Entrance and Driveway
2. Lobby
3. Dining Hall
4. Kitchen
5. Service/Storage
6. Cocktail Lounge
7. Administration
8. Planter
9. Lobby & TV Room
10. Swimming Pool
11. Pool Deck Area
12. Planting Areas
13. Guest Rooms
14. Kiddie Pool/Sand Box
15. Recreation Room
16. Guest Parking
17. Service Parking
18. Intracoastal Waterway

The Diplomat Hotel was across the street from the Envoy Motel. The enormous, concrete canopy at the hotel entrance provided a visual connection between the two facilities. From the side, the shape of this feature seemed triangular, an inversion of the Envoy's giant *V*'s. As guests approached the entrance, however, it became apparent that the canopy was actually in the shape of a hyperbolic paraboloid. The structure's span extended fifty feet beyond the driveway in one direction and fifty feet through the plate-glass wall into the hotel's lobby in the other. Astonishingly, the entire concrete shell was balanced on only two points. The firm's structural engineer, Jules Channing, helped me design it. Daring and dramatic, the canopy was an unforgettable statement. Its unusual form was exciting to behold, and guests certainly knew where to enter the hotel.

Diplomat Hotel, Hollywood, Florida, 1957–58 (demolished). Rendering.

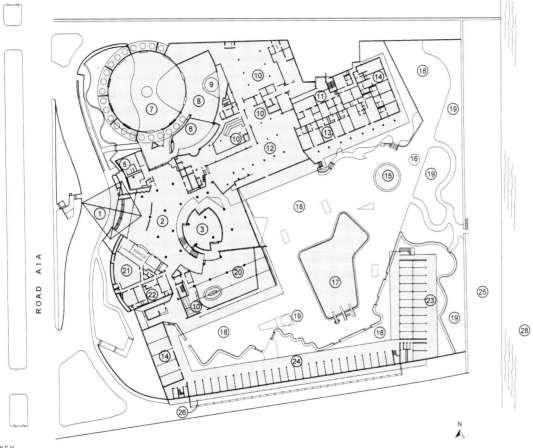

N

Diplomat Hotel, Hollywood, Florida, 1957–58 (demolished). Main lobby. The facility's decorating scheme featured materials from over fifteen countries, including volcanic rock from the ruins at Pompeii (*above*); ground-floor plan (*left*).

KEY

1. Entrance and Driveway
2. Lobby
3. Main Lobby
4. Elevators
5. Public Toilets
6. La Petite Chose

7. Les Ambassadeurs
8. Café Crystal
9. Movable Stage
10. Kitchens
11. Services, Storage
12. Bon Appetite Room

13. Guest Rooms
14. Studio Rooms
15. Kiddie Pool
16. Sandbox
17. Swimming
18. Pool Deck Area

19. Planting Areas
20. Tack Room Bar
21. General Offices
22. Private Offices
23. Cabanas
24. Cabanas and Balcony

25. Beach Area
26. Underground Parking
27. Service Parking
28. Atlantic Ocean

The materials I used to decorate the areas surrounding the canopy enhanced the sense of splendor and excitement. I again chose glass mosaic tiles—here in shimmering aqua, yellow, and orange—to adorn the wall just north of the hotel's entrance. In the 1950s, leisure time was informal, festive, fun, and colorful. Multihued tiles were a wonderfully appropriate way of incorporating this celebratory spirit into a building dedicated to relaxation and escape.

I punctuated the white walls leading up to the entrance with thin columns of gold anodized aluminum, a revolutionary product in the 1950s. The thin columns gave the façade a lighter appearance, broke up the long expanse of white wall, and balanced the bold tiles. I also used gold anodized aluminum railings on the balconies along the guest tower's western side. Although structurally unnecessary, the colorful tiles and aluminum columns were visual luxuries, added solely to make life sparkle and glitter.

Once inside, guests found themselves in a large, impressively decorated space. The interior designer, Franklin Hughes, con-

Diplomat Hotel, Hollywood, Florida, 1957–58 (demolished). Gold anodized aluminum ornamented the lobby's hanging staircase (*left*) and the guest tower's balcony railings (*right*).

The Diplomat's glamorous image and luxurious accommodations made it a much sought-after resort destination.

tinued the white, gold, and aqua palette throughout the public areas.[1] He illuminated the lobby with a magnificent crystal and aluminum chandelier, the last one to be imported from Cuba before Fidel Castro nationalized the industry. A grand staircase made entirely of gold anodized aluminum floated just beyond the glamorous light fixture. The staircase design evolved from the more modest Giller Building stair concept. Together, these spectacular suspended features elicited awed reactions from hotel guests.

Adjacent to the lobby were two stylish lounges. La Petite Chose, with its black silk walls, crimson ceiling, and pencil spotlights, provided the perfect setting for a romantic start to the evening or for a relaxing cocktail at the end of the day. The Tack

Room, which overlooked the pool deck, was a popular place to have lunch. After broadcasting equipment was installed in the space, the Tack Room became known as the "springboard to fame" for aspiring stars.

For an elegant dining experience, the Diplomat's Les Ambassadeurs was unparalleled. This formal salon was located in a circular concrete structure at the northern end of the hotel building that shared space with a supper club, the Café Cristal, where great entertainers of the era often performed.

By this point in my career, the circle had become one of my favorite ways of transforming a basic structure into something distinctive. The form was an important stylistic element in the design of this entertainment wing. In addition to the large circular coves in the ceiling of the main corridor encircling the ballroom and supper club, I domed the roof and punctured its perimeter with large, round holes, allowing natural light to filter into the interior spaces. The same detail could be seen along the top of the guest tower, providing a unifying element. The curved walls and concrete circles functioned both as ornament and structure.

This picture was part of a fashion spread that appeared in *Harper's Bazaar* in January 1959. According to the telegram, "the doll is dazzled by diplomat's gold staircase."

Diplomat Hotel, Hollywood, Florida, 1957–58 (demolished). Interior view, entertainment wing. I repeated the large concrete circles at the top of the guest tower as coves in the ceiling of the entertainment wing.

The Diplomat complex exemplified my continual desire to design a building that was different from the one next door. It was a philosophy that Sam Friedland understood. We broke ground for the golf course in 1956 on Sam's sixtieth birthday. As he dug the shovel into the ground, he said that the start of the project was his birthday gift. Sam was very proud of the Diplomat. Although he had built a few other hotels a number of years earlier, I think he considered this leisure complex his masterpiece. You certainly do not build Diplomat resorts everyday.

Diplomat Hotel and Country Club, Hollywood, Florida, 1956–58 (demolished). Photograph, ca. 1958. Aerial view. The country club and golf course are in the foreground, and the hotel (*right center*) and the motel (*far right*) are in the background. In the late 1990s, the original Diplomat Hotel was replaced by the Westin Diplomat Resort and Spa, a 39-story, 998-room luxury hotel.

NORTH SHORE COMMUNITY CENTER

The plan of the North Shore Community Center reflects my continued interest in sculptured concrete. The City of Miami Beach hired me to design the open-air facility in the North Beach area to host dances, performances, and other special events for residents and tourists. The central space had to be completely free of permanent structures in order to accommodate the wide range of civic activities. Thus I focused my creative energies on the perimeter elements.

The pavilion's modernistic design is composed of circles and curves. Although the stage is the largest structure, the two entrances function as the community center's focal points. Large, cantilevered, disk-shaped canopies mark each entrance. They are supported and counterbalanced by tall columns. Since the narrow, curved columns are the canopies' only means of support, the disks appear to hover above the perimeter walls. I placed these wide canopies rather low, so that people walking under them are aware that they are entering an enclosed space. In contrast, those leaving the protection of the canopies immediately find themselves in view of the expansive sky. As with the Diplomat Hotel's hyperbolic paraboloid, the striking, sculptural quality of these canopies leaves no question as to where the entrances are located.

The high, concrete wall encircling the amphitheater continues the curvilinear theme. The two entrance towers, a third tower of curved columns from which a spotlight is projected, and the stage are the only elements that punctuate the circular wall. Rounded concrete layers decorate the sides of the stage. The staggering of these layers amplifies the sound and provides screening for backstage preparations. Behind the stage are small dressing and storage rooms. A precast concrete pattern that resembles quarter moons, or smiles and frowns, adorns the sides of the proscenium. This detail offers texture and contrast, and serves as an inexpensive, low-maintenance means of decorating the stage. Terrazzo, laid in circular patterns, covers the floor of the large, open central area. Although the center has minimal wall space relative to its size, the flexible design is functional and unique, making it a favorite gathering place. During the winter season, the community space is packed with residents and tourists dancing under the stars, cooled by the balmy ocean breezes.

North Shore Community Center, Miami Beach, 1961. Photograph, 2001.

North Shore Community Center, Miami Beach, 1961. Renderings (*left*); photograph, 2001 (*below*). The City of Miami Beach is in the process of designating the former North Shore Community Center—now known as the North Shore Bandshell—as a historic site.

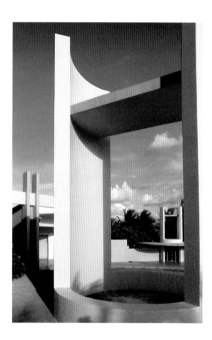

North Shore Community Center, Miami Beach, 1961. Photograph, ca. 1965. Aerial view. Collins Avenue (Route A1A) is to the west, and the beach and Atlantic Ocean are to the east.

SESS

ALIANZA
PARA EL PRO
USA

MIAMI MODERNISM EXPORTED: The Alliance for Progress

On February 2, 1962, I received a phone call from the Agency for International Development of the U.S. State Department (U.S. AID) in Washington, D.C. The caller wanted to know if I would be interested in designing and supervising the construction of the National School Program in the Republic of Panama. The project was part of President John F. Kennedy's recently announced ten-year, $20-billion pan-American initiative, the Alliance for Progress/Alianza por el Progresso. Like many Americans, I had read news stories about the Alliance, but I never expected that I would be creating elegant Miami hotels and homes one day and the next serving my country by designing education facilities in Latin America.

The Alliance for Progress sought to stimulate Latin American social and economic development in an effort to ensure long-term stability and raise standards of living in the region. The Alliance was a cooperative effort in which all participants were peers. The Latin American host countries determined the specific needs of their people and supplied land and labor, while the United States provided capital and technical aid. A significant portion of the program focused on creating a healthier population, increasing literacy, and building infrastructure. I was enthusiastic about the opportunity to contribute to such a significant enterprise and excited by the prospect of new architectural challenges.

Prototype elementary school, Panama, 1962. Rendering.

Twelve days after that initial 1962 phone call, I arrived in Panama City to begin the Alliance for Progress work. It was, coincidentally, also my forty-fourth birthday. The Panamanian president, Don Roberto F. Chiari, had already promised his citizens that, with the assistance of the United States, schools would be built quickly. The Ministry of Education's plan for a national school system called for the construction of small primary schools in all the rural areas, primary and middle schools in all the towns, and primary, middle, and high schools in all the cities. Just as I was realizing the complexities of blending U.S. bidding procedures with Panamanian design and building practices, President Chiari invited me to his palace to insist that we break ground for the first primary school within six weeks. As was the case with many of my earlier projects, I needed to create, quickly and cost-effectively, a visually arresting building that responded to tropical conditions. The difficulty was determining how to make a basic, functional structure convey elements of good design.

In order to best meet these requirements, I turned to the one-floor elementary school plan that had been common in the United States since the 1940s. I organized the school as a complex of five, single-story concrete buildings connected to one another with covered walkways. The floor plan was specifically oriented to take advantage of natural breezes. Materials like concrete and glass were used in ways that had become standard in my "contemporary" buildings. Cross-ventilation was of paramount importance. Wherever possible, rows of glass

Norman M. Giller showing Panamanian president Roberto F. Chiari and his ministers a rendering of the first Panamanian elementary school built under the Alliance for Progress initiative. All plans and documentation had to be bilingual, and all measurements had to be in English and metric. Although Miami's population today is predominantly Latin, in the early 1960s finding someone who could translate architectural terminology into Spanish was extremely difficult.

jalousie windows, new to Panama, lined opposing walls. I extended the eaves of the gently pitched roofs to provide protection from rain and sun, and, on one side, to shelter the access corridor. This sleek, overhanging detail was culled from my suburban home designs of the mid-1950s. Typically, I relied on concrete for structure and embellishment, adding landscaped plazas and interior courtyards to the schools when possible. I worked on the plans around the clock, and construction of the first primary school began within five weeks.

The design of the Collegio Jose D. Moscote, one of the first high schools I planned for Panama City, further sought to blend "contemporary" techniques with local conditions. The campus included sixty classrooms, laboratories, vocational facilities, and a library. I again relied upon a vocabulary of covered walkways, landscaped courtyards, glass jalousies, and overhanging roofs, but on a larger scale. I inexpensively incorporated rhythm and movement into the otherwise boxy structure by capping the roof with a series of arches that mimic the form of clay barrel tiles. Clay is abundant in Panama, and, for centuries, workmen had been shaping clay roof tiles by laying a slab of the softened material across their thighs. Taking advantage of the local supply of clay and skilled craftsmen, the school's undulating roof was made of clay barrel tiles sealed with a layer of cement.

Shortly after the education project got underway, U.S. AID and the Panamanian government asked me to assume responsibility for the facilities of Panama's National Health Program. Many of the same design principles, materials, and building techniques utilized for the schools were applied to the design of the clinics and hospitals. Ultimately, I was involved in the design and construction of fifteen health care centers, including the 300-bed regional hospital in Aguadulce and a 600-bed psychiatric hospital in the Central Provinces.

As my involvement with the Alliance progressed, U.S. AID invited me to oversee the development of similar education and health-care buildings in Nicaragua, El Salvador, Colombia, and Brazil. I spent much of the 1960s supervising these projects using the designs I made for Panama as our models. My associates and I would serve first as architectural and engineering consultants, then as designers, and finally as construction managers.

Much of my success in working for the Alliance was due to a policy my American employees and I referred to as "diplomatic architecture." In order to design structures that truly met people's needs, I often traveled from site to site, frequently by jeep or boat, sometimes on horseback, in a canoe, or on foot. I met with presidents, peasants, and every type of person in between. Throughout my visits, I encountered many practices and routines that differed from familiar American customs. Although I might have been aware of another technique, I believed I was there to offer guidance, not to "Americanize" the working methods and cultures of the local communities.

Since funding for the Alliance projects came from the U.S. government, however, the work, contractually, had to be done according to the laws and procedures that I had always followed. My employees and I soon learned that making courteous, carefully worded suggestions to our Latin American colleagues was the most effective way to earn respect and get high-quality work accomplished.

Collegio Jose D. Moscote, Panama City, 1962. Two views of the high school's covered walkways, plazas, and vaulted roofs.

RIO GRANDE DO NORTE
GABINETE DO GOVERNADOR

Ofício n. 46 /GE

NATAL

Em 27 janeiro de 1966

Senhor Engenheiro,

Na oportunidade em que me afasto do
Govêrno do Estado, por ter concluído o mandato de que
fui investido, desejo externar o meu agradecimento a
essa conceituada firma pela colaboração útil e compe -
tente que prestou ao programa de educação realizado pe
lo meu govêrno com a ajuda financeira da Aliança Para
o Progresso.

Devo registrar o bom entendimento -
que sempre marcou as relações dessa firma sob sua es
clarecida chefia, com a Secretaria de Educação e equi
pe técnicas, conjugando esforços para o melhor provei-
to das metas recomendadas no Convênio e que afinal se
concretizaram com o esperado êxito.

Com a renovação do meu aprêço, apre-
sento minhas saudações.

ALUÍZIO ALVES
GOVERNADOR

Ilmo. Sr.
EDWARD A. CUDLIPP
M.D. Engenheiro Chefe
Norman M. Giller & Associados

By the mid-1960s, norman m. giller & associates had six offices throughout Central and South America. Each office manager would hire local
professionals to oversee development of the projects. This picture
shows the team that worked in the firm's office in northeast Brazil.

ESTA CONSTRUCCION
ES EL RESULTADO DE LA COOPERACION
ENTRE LOS PUEBLOS DE LOS
ESTADOS UNIDOS DE AMERICA
Y
PANAMA
ESTA OBRA ES UNA DEMOSTRACION CONCRETA
DE LA AMISTAD Y LA UNION QUE EXISTE ENTRE
LOS ESTADOS UNIDOS Y PANAMA

Signs like this one
could be seen on
construction sites
throughout Panama
in the early 1960s.
The schools in the
most rural areas often
included faculty living
quarters as an incen-
tive for teachers to
accept positions.

This billboard was posted on a main boulevard in Rio de Janeiro the day after President Kennedy had successfully resolved the Cuban Missile Crisis. The showdown with Fidel Castro had made him a hero in Brazil yet again.

The technical assistance my team and I provided for the design and construction of schools and health centers helped ensure that the goals of the Alliance for Progress were met. These facilities, along with the countless others built through the program, were directly responsible for the venture's considerable, tangible achievements. As health and education levels of millions of Latin Americans improved, the standard of living across the hemisphere rose. As anticipated, the undertaking significantly helped to lower infant mortality rates and raise life expectancy. Governments were inspired to substantially increase funding for education and health care. The massive construction effort spurred the development of new industries. Countless unskilled workers received on-the-job training while skilled workers familiarized themselves with more efficient procedures and materials.[1]

My involvement with this international program gave me a tremendous amount of personal satisfaction. I have always felt grateful for the opportunity to see my designs being used to help people better their lives. The Alliance projects certainly were the most rewarding of my architectural career.

The Brazilian people named one of the teacher's colleges I designed after President John F. Kennedy. Robert Kennedy, U.S. attorney general at the time, flew to Natal, Brazil, to dedicate the school. The crowd was so large that Kennedy and the Brazilian dignitaries had to stand on the roof of one of the covered walkways to ensure that everyone could see them.

COLLEGE OF BUSINESS ADMINISTRATION AND
COLLEGE OF EDUCATION, FLORIDA ATLANTIC UNIVERSITY

The structures I designed in the 1960s appear very different from their predecessors. As the decade progressed, an interest in monumentality and timelessness overtook the preference for weightlessness and whimsy. Megastructures became fashionable. Sleek walls of glass gave way to thick, rough concrete surfaces. Bulky, geometric shapes arranged in repetitive, highly ordered patterns replaced fluid organic details. Interiors were made to seem enclosed and inward-looking. Artificial rather than natural light illuminated internal spaces.[1]

The grand, imposing later works of architects Louis I. Kahn, Mies van der Rohe, and Le Corbusier helped to inspire this re-direction. For Kahn, "monumentality in architecture" described "a spiritual quality inherent in a structure which conveys the feelings of its eternity, that it cannot be added to or changed."[2] One manner of achieving the effect was to invigorate Classical elements with a Modern handling of form and material. Mies van der Rohe's glass-enclosed New National Gallery of Art (Berlin, 1962) is an abstracted Greek temple, complete with carefully ordered steel columns, a raised base, and an immense overhanging steel entablature.

Monumentality could also be attained through the use of massive unfinished concrete forms. The robust walls, hefty columns, and ordered geometric shapes of Le Corbusier's

College of Business Administration and College of Education, Florida Atlantic University, Boca Raton, Florida, 1965.

concrete Monastery of La Tourette (Lyons, 1953–60) evoke permanence and immutability. The raw concrete cladding is textured and irregular, evidence of the process by which the material took shape. Heavy, concrete buildings that employed Le Corbusier's preference for the *béton brut* (raw concrete) finishing technique came to be referred to as "Brutalist." The metaphor of structure as fortress rather than open pavilion was deemed especially appropriate for public buildings.

Just as architectural trends changed in the 1960s, so, too, did my client base. As the large companies and sprawling communities formed during the postwar boom matured, both the private and public sectors found themselves with the means and the need for more comprehensive facilities. In 1968, I designed an enormous suburban department store for J. C. Penny Corporation. It was the type of large-scale commission by the type of large-scale corporation that a decade before did not exist.

After operating for almost two decades, my firm had evolved as well. The range of projects completed during the 1950s and early 1960s gave us the design and planning experience that corporate and government clients found attractive. At the same time, managing regional projects as well as those overseas forced me to rely more heavily on my technical director, Dutch architect Jan Smit. His European training is evident in the sophisticated corporate structures of the mid-1960s and 1970s.

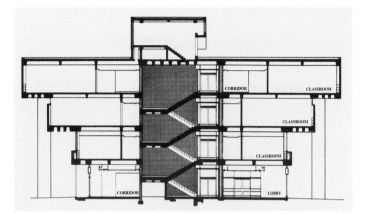

College of Education administrative building and shared Classroom Building, Florida Atlantic University, Boca Raton, Florida, 1965.

Classroom Building, Florida Atlantic University, Boca Raton, Florida, 1965. Cross-section.

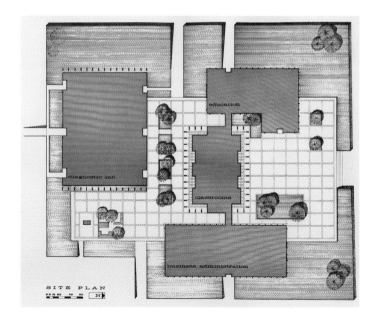

Finally, as the complexity of my new projects grew, I was able to be more selective about those I accepted. While the volume of commissions decreased, the qualitative scope of each one increased considerably.

Although I was still obtaining commissions for motels and homes, by about 1962 I began dedicating more time to planning hospitals, schools, government offices, and business facilities—the exact building types that called for more monumental treatment. Whereas my leisure-industry buildings needed to be eye-catching and expressive, my institutional, corporate, and educational structures were designed to embody a sense of seriousness and stability.

College of Business Administration and College of Education, Florida Atlantic University, Boca Raton, Florida, 1965. Site plan. The FAU campus sits on a parcel of land that was once an Army Air Force base. Coincidentally, while employed by the Corps of Engineers during World War II, I had worked on the design of the base. In 1965, as I was looking through the plans of the original buildings, I discovered blueprints with my name on them.

The classrooms, offices, and laboratories I designed for the College of Education and the College of Business Administration at the newly established Florida Atlantic University in Boca Raton suggest this more sedate vocabulary. Using dense, somber materials in a highly disciplined manner, I designed a bold facility to anchor the northern end of the campus's main axis.[3] Right angles, rather than free-form details, predominate the geometry of the four-building complex. The rectilinear structures sit on a vast, gridded platform. The conversation pits embedded into the brick plaza echo the shape of their stately neighbors. The placement of simple rectangular benches and planters encourages students to congregate in these areas between classes. The exterior of each building features a classically inspired textured concrete entablature supported by regularly spaced, rectangular concrete columns.

Despite the structures' weighty, reserved forms, the composition still incorporates the play of textures and volumes that I have always enjoyed. Areas of coarse, exposed aggregate contrast with smooth concrete latticework. Slender rectangular columns support bulky concrete overhangs, the undersides of which are coffered by square concrete waffle holes. The open yet intimate communal conversation pits counter the imposing concrete buildings.

While each college has its own administrative facility, the centrally placed Classroom Building is shared. As the building essentially functions as the heart of academic life, I designed it to rise above the other single-story structures. For the sake of cohesion, the Classroom Building is topped by an entablature and encircled by columns. Each of its stories, however, is pro-gressively recessed, giving the structure a distinctive, inverted pyramid form.

The size of the floors, reinforced by the juxtaposition of concrete and glass, challenge the typical orientation of "heavy supporting delicate." The top floor contains large rooms for lectures and audiovisual presentations. Thick concrete walls enclose this story, blocking all natural light. Medium-sized traditional-style classrooms can be found on the third level. A row of ribbon windows and striated concrete walls make the exterior of this floor seem less impenetrable. Seminars are conducted in the small classrooms that comprise the second story. Here, I reduced the concrete to a single band and enveloped the walls in glass. The ground floor is as open as possible to facilitate the sudden and significant flow of people that occurs when classes change. Glass panels encase the small offices and rooms at the building's base. Concrete walls have been eliminated. The entrance to the building is not obvious, a nod to Brutalist works. Placing all of the same-sized rooms on the same floors enabled the structure to express its different internal functions, and helped orient students and professors.

The Classroom Building's wide top and recessed lower levels recalls Le Corbusier's Monastery of La Tourette, yet the overall effect is much lighter. While the bulky, windowless fourth story appears poised to crush the airy, glass-enclosed floors below it, the arrangement actually allows each overhanging floor to protect the areas beneath it from the region's blazing sunshine and intense rainstorms. Attributes like this gave the complex a subtle bit of regional flair.

INTERAMERICAN NATIONAL BANK

In the mid-1960s, I began a second, concurrent career—that of a banker. As my experience with the Rubiyat Hotel in 1956 proved, financing is one of the most important factors in bringing a development to fruition. Without an owner's ability to pay for the construction, the building design is only paper architecture. This concern aroused an interest in banking quite early in my architectural career. I knew founding a bank would enable me to understand loan criteria from the lender's point of view as well as from the borrower's, a perspective invaluable to my design process.

After serving on the board of directors of a local bank for several years, I decided in 1963 that it was time to organize a bank of my own. I gathered a group of partners and began researching areas of need in Miami-Dade County. Sunny Isles, the very area where I had designed my first motel, kept topping my list of appropriate locations. Launching my banking career in virtually the same location where I had launched my architectural career almost twenty years earlier was a happy coincidence. After completing an exhaustive application process, my partners and I received a telegram on August 24, 1964, from the U.S. comptroller of the currency granting us a charter to form a new national bank.

The first InterAmerican National Bank office opened in a rehabilitated storefront building in January 1965. I served as the president and chairman of the board. As an architect-banker,

InterAmerican National Bank, Sunny Isles, 1966.

I often encouraged officers at other financial institutions to become cognizant of good design practices. By establishing architectural standards, design excellence became another factor in determining the economic viability of a project.

Sunny Isles proved to be a growing, active community, and within a few months the bank's board of directors determined that a larger facility was needed. They purchased a waterfront property across the street from the storefront office and commissioned norman m. giller & associates to create a new, freestanding bank building.

The design of the InterAmerican Bank structure needed to convey strength and security, an image important to both the banking industry and its customers. I also wanted to take advantage of the beautiful waterfront location and have the building reflect, in some way, the Florida lifestyle. Taking a cue from Mies's New National Gallery of Art, I devised a single-story, glass-enclosed pavilion surrounded by a series of bold rectangular, concrete columns and topped with a wide precast concrete entablature. Rectangular concrete shapes run along the edge of the roof band, referencing the columns below and giving a sense of uprightness to the otherwise low, horizontal structure. The white stucco diamond-dust finish that covers the columns and entablature subtly sparkles in the Florida sunshine. The smoky tint applied to the plate-glass windows contrasts with the white stucco elements on the exterior and helps shield the interior from the sun. The entire structure rests on a large, square platform raised several feet above grade, which

InterAmerican National Bank, Sunny Isles, 1966. The teller counter inside the bank building. InterAmerican National Bank was named after Interama, a nearby Latin American–themed exposition that was never realized. In 1968, InterAmerican National Bank merged with Jefferson National Bank and took its name. When Colonial Bancorp purchased Jefferson in 1997, the Sunny Isles branch was closed.

anchors the building in the surrounding landscaped environment. A range of materials, including Travertine, black marble, cork, wool, and Formica, decorates the interior spaces. Earth-toned décor combined with a "humanly scaled" ceiling height creates a warm, welcoming, yet professional environment.

Although only one story was built, the structure was designed to support the addition of five more floors of office space. The dynamic forms, theatrical cantilevers, and bold palettes commonly found in my other projects yield here to right angles, Classical proportions, and neutral colors in an effort to express stability and permanence. A commitment to reduced ornamentation, truth to materials, and bringing the outdoors in remains.

While active at the bank, I became very involved in the economic development of Sunny Isles. Lessons I had learned while planning communities for military and private developers gave me insights into the needs of a young municipality. Over the years, I worked with other civic leaders to help plan and secure funding for the Sunny Isles' water and sewage systems, street-lighting projects, landscaping improvements, and other public works. Partially inspired by my experiences with the Alliance for Progress, my work with the Sunny Isles community was an extension of my professional role as planner and architect.

InterAmerican National Bank, Sunny Isles, 1966. Rear elevation, as seen from across the waterway. The entrance on the waterfront side allowed patrons to bank by boat, a service unique to InterAmerican Bank at the time.

U.S. Senator Claude Pepper cutting the ribbon at the official dedication ceremony of InterAmerican National Bank, February 20, 1965. The ribbon was made of thirty, one-hundred-dollar bills taped together. I politely asked the senator to make sure to cut the ribbon between the hundred-dollar bills rather than through them. He was very accommodating.

EASTERN AIRLINES CAFETERIA

Like that of the InterAmerican National Bank building, the design of the Eastern Airlines Cafeteria combines Classical details with a subtropical modernist twist. When Eastern Airlines officials hired me to design the structure in 1967, they were faced with an intriguing problem. The company needed a cafeteria large enough to serve lunch to their 2,400 employees but did not have the budget to build a facility that could feed all of them simultaneously.

In order to resolve this dilemma, I incorporated a time-study analysis into my design process. The study sought to determine the smallest amount of space that could accommodate the service needs of thousands of hungry employees. First, I examined the time it took the average employee to choose, pay for, and eat his or her lunch. From this data, I determined that rather than having all the employees dine at noon, three shifts of eight hundred employees each would enter the cafeteria at 12:00 p.m., 12:30 p.m., and 1:00 p. m. To prevent long lines, each shift would be broken down further into four groups entering at ten-minute intervals. By staggering the shifts, and the groups within the shifts, a 600-seat cafeteria would be able to serve all 2,400 employees in an hour and a half. The cost of this smaller cafeteria fell comfortably within the budgetary limitations.

Once I established the schedule and determined the size of the building, I began organizing the structure's interior. In order

Eastern Airlines Cafeteria, Miami, 1967.

Eastern Airlines Cafeteria, Miami, 1967. West elevation, exit.

Eastern Airlines Cafeteria, Miami, 1967. Traffic flow chart.

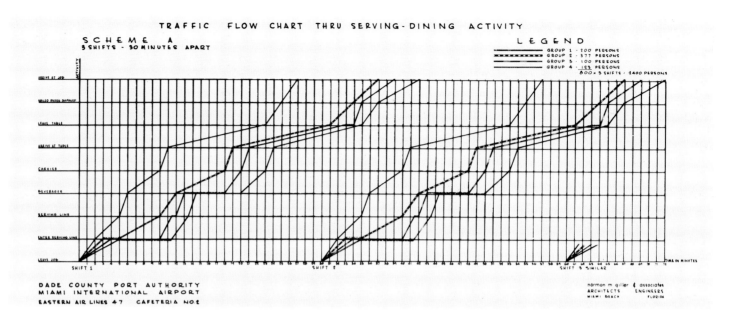

to facilitate traffic flow, I placed the entrance and food service area on the south side of the building, and the seating area and the exit on the west side. I broke the food service area into several distinct stations. Rather than waiting in a single cafeteria line, employees walked directly to the sandwich station or the salad bar or the hot foods area and then proceeded to the cashier. Once they were finished with their meals, employees left their trays on the kitchen-bound conveyor belt that ran along the perimeter of the dining section.

The dining hall's inward orientation and exterior ornament reflect corporate preferences at the time. In contrast to the expansive glass walls of the InterAmerican National Bank building, the concrete walls of the Eastern Airlines Cafeteria are interrupted only by narrow, vertical windows and glass doors. The single-story building rests on a raised podium and is surrounded by a colonnaded loggia. The platform doubles as a planter. Encircling the building with greenery softens its hard, perpendicular lines and creates a transition between natural and constructed. The colonnade further frames the structure, giving depth to the elevation. The white diamond-dust stucco columns and entablature, and black, slightly recessed border also add dimension. By combining scientific study with clean, modern design, I was able to create a graceful facility that comfortably met the requirements of its owners and users.

Eastern Airlines Cafeteria, Miami, 1967. Rendering. North elevation. The asymmetrically placed windows and rooftop equipment screen counterbalance the building's Classically inspired colonnade and elevated platform. The horizontal band passing across the grouping of windows expresses the conveyor system that circumscribes the cafeteria.

Epilogue

I remember midcentury Miami as a modern city, full of fresh ideas and exciting opportunities. Thousands of transplants eager to start new lives in an optimistic, postwar world had begun to call it home. Thousands more tourists were visiting each season to be cooled by Miami's subtropical breezes, sunbathe along its spectacular beaches, and swim in its beautiful ocean. Perhaps more than anything, Miami Modernist architecture was designed to reflect and respond to the area's sensational natural environment. True to Modernist form, my midcentury designs were influenced as much by what surrounded a structure as by what needed to be placed within it. Open, airy buildings, with their large expanses of glass, permanent indoor planters, landscaped patios, and open-plan spaces blurred the distinction between indoors and outdoors, and encouraged a newly informal lifestyle that did the same. The clean lines and pared-down "contemporary" details that adorned Miami's colorful, new oceanfront buildings seemed shockingly refreshing, especially to northern eyes used to the heavy, dark buildings common to older, overcrowded urban areas. And then there was the year-round green. The sunshine never seemed to end, and I wanted my buildings to let people take advantage of this to the fullest extent. While the days of hyperbolic paraboloids and themed motels are long gone, the "good life" that this modernistic Miami architecture helped to create continues to thrive. This is, conceivably, MiMo's greatest contribution.

By the early 1970s, my role in the firm had changed. When my son Ira joined norman m. giller & associates in 1972, he began to take over much of the design process and day-to-day operations. As senior partner, I had the opportunity to spend more time in public service and as a banker. In 1974, I formed the Concerned Citizens of Northeast Dade County to persuade government officials to undertake the type of public works projects critical to the development of Sunny Isles. I also spent fourteen years lobbying officials to build a bridge and causeway connecting the area to the mainland. When these projects were finally completed in 1983, the Florida State Legislature named the Sunny Isles bridge in my honor. The Norman M. Giller Bridge is one of the few bridges in the United States named after a living architect.

In the late 1970s, I began lobbying the City of Miami Beach to establish an independent architectural review board in order to advocate growth based on the principles of good design and urban planning. The seven-person board, consisting of design and planning professionals as well as representatives of the community, would review all building plans to ensure that each project would contribute to the city's quality of life. By 1984, a Design Review Board had been appointed and its guidelines regarding building scale, orientation, and ornamentation began to upgrade the caliber of design throughout the city. I held the honor of serving as the board's chairman for nine years.

The Design Review Board continues to play a pivotal role in the development of Miami Beach.

As a result of my passion for history and my Jewish heritage, I dedicated a significant amount of time in the 1990s to spearheading the effort to establish a permanent home for the Jewish Museum of Florida. Located in a restored South Beach synagogue building listed on the National Register of Historic Places, the museum opened to much fanfare in 1995. My firm completed the renovations that transformed the structure into a museum facility. In 1998, the National Trust for Historic Preservation awarded the firm the prestigious National Preservation Award. The firm norman m. giller & associates was renamed Giller & Giller, Inc., in 1992 and remains actively involved in the development of South Florida today.

Selected Postwar Commissions

Dates reflect the year the project was commissioned.

1946 • Congregation Beth Tfilah, Miami Beach

1947 • Miracle Minit Man Automatic Car Wash, Miami Beach
• Morey Giller Apartments, Miami Beach
• Pine Tree Lake Apartments, Miami Beach
• Writing Studio, Sholom Asch, Miami Beach

1948 • Copa City Night Club (with Norman Bel Geddes), Miami Beach
• Feathershave Safety Razor Plant, Miami
• Mal Marshall Guayabera Shirt Factory, Miami
• Shapiro Residence, Miami Beach

1949 • Ocean Palm Motel, Sunny Isles
• Ruby Lane Dress Stores, Gainesville and Ocala, Florida

1950 • Apartment Buildings, Federal Public Housing Administration and Miami Beach Housing Authority, Miami Beach
• Knoxon Drive-In Hotel, Miami
• Masonic Temple, Miami Beach
• Sandy Shores Motel, Sunny Isles

1951 • Bali Motel, Sunny Isles
• Coral Seas Motel, Sunny Isles
• Driftwood Motel, Sunny Isles
• Fountainhead Motel, Sunny Isles
• Hotel Bombay, Miami Beach
• Magic Isle Motel, Sunny Isles
• Norman M. Giller Residence, Miami Beach
• Tahiti Motel, Sunny Isles

1952 • Hillel House, University of Miami, Coral Gables, Florida
• Juno Beach Motel, Juno Beach, Florida
• Neptune Resort Motel, Sunny Isles

1953 • Monterrey Motel, Miami Beach
• Tangiers Motel, Sunny Isles

1954 • Beverly Hotel, Las Vegas (unbuilt)
• Blue Marlin Motel, Key West
• Chateau Motel, Sunny Isles
• Coral Way Village, F&R Housing Corporation, Miami
• Food Fair Stores, various cities in Florida
• Thivierge Motel, Montreal, Canada (unbuilt)
• Thunderbird Motel, Sunny Isles

1955 • Alpha Epsilon Phi Sorority House, Gainesville, Florida
• Calloway Gardens Motel, Pine Mountain, Georgia
• Food Fair Shopping Centers, various cities in Florida
• Hudelson Hotel, Toronto, Canada (unbuilt)
• Pitney-Bowes Building, Jacksonville, Florida
• Sebring Hills Housing Development, Sebring, Florida
• Suez Motel, Sunny Isles
• Sunrise Supermarkets, Long Island and Brooklyn, New York

1956 • Diplomat Hotel and Country Club, Hollywood, Florida
• Homestead Air Force Base Capehart Housing, Homestead, Florida
• Key West Naval Air Station Family Housing, Key West, Florida
• Patrick Air Force Base Housing, Cape Canaveral, Florida
• Rubiyat Hotel, Bal Harbour, Florida

1957
- Carillon Hotel, Miami Beach
- Giller Building, Miami Beach
- Singapore Hotel, Bal Harbour, Florida

1958
- Berman Motel, Atlantic City, New Jersey
- Bowliseum Bowling Alley, Orlando, Florida
- Crossroads Bowling Alley, St. Petersburg, Florida
- Executive Motor Hotel, Richmond, Virginia
- Sahara Motor Hotel, Cleveland, Ohio

1959
- The Giller Plan: A Comprehensive Redevelopment Plan for South Beach, Miami Beach
- Jet Engine Maintenance Shop, U.S. Naval Air Station, Jacksonville, Florida

1960
- Aristocrat Motor Hotel, Hot Springs, Arkansas
- Haldon Homes, Lauderdale Lakes, Florida
- Key West Naval Air Station Capehart Family Housing, Key West

1961
- American Eiffel Tower, Miami Beach (unbuilt)
- Civic Auditorium, Cocoa Beach, Florida
- North Shore Community Center, Miami Beach
- Research Center and Clean Room Laboratory, U.S. Army Corps of Engineers, Cape Canaveral Missile Test Center, Florida

1962
- Cartography and Mineral Resources Building, Panama City, Panama
- Hobbs Motor Hotel and Convention Center, Hobbs, New Mexico
- Integrated Health Center Facilities (fifteen), various communities in Panama

- National School Construction Program (forty-five schools), various communities in Panama
- National School Construction Program, Pernambuco, Brazil
- Psychiatric Hospital, Los Santos, Panama
- Regional General Hospital, Aguadulce, Panama

1963
- City of Cocoa Police Station and Court House, Cocoa, Florida
- National School Construction Program, various communities in Nicaragua

1964
- Boy Scouts of America Administration Building, Miami
- National Health Center Construction Program (twenty-four centers), Rio Grande do Norte, Brazil
- National School Construction Program, Rio Grande do Norte, Brazil

1965
- Florida Atlantic University, Boca Raton, Florida
- NASA Visitor Center, Design Invitational, Cape Kennedy, Florida
- National Health Center Construction Program, various communities in El Salvador

1966
- Family Housing, Howard Air Force Base, Panama Canal Zone
- InterAmerican National Bank, Sunny Isles

1967
- Air Terminal Facility, Tocumen, Panama
- Eastern Airlines Cafeteria, Miami International Airport, Miami

1968
- 801 Building, Miami Beach
- J. C. Penny Co. Department Store, Dadeland Shopping Mall, Miami
- Maule Industries Cement Plant Office Building, Miami
- Miami Gardens Elementary School, North Miami

Notes

Introduction

1. "Motel Row," *Practical Builder* (1956): 30.
2. Quoted in Marcus, *Design in the Fifties*, 117. See also Jackson, *'Contemporary,'* 39–43. Almost twenty years later, Robert Venturi, Denise Scott Brown, and Steven Izenour expressed a similar sentiment when they stated that Modern architects "build for Man rather than for men." Venturi, Brown, and Izenour, *Learning from Las Vegas*, 106.

Technologies

1. Le Corbusier, *Towards a New Architecture*, 133; citations are to the Dover edition. See also Murray Fraiser and Joe Kerr, "Motopia: Cities, Cars and Architecture," in Wollen and Kerr, *Autopia*, 316.
2. Le Corbusier, *Towards a New Architecture*, 240.
3. This idea is developed further in Robert M. Craig, "Transportation Imagery and Streamline Moderne Architecture," in Jennings, *Roadside America*, 15–28.
4. Hine, *Populuxe*, 18.
5. Karal Ann Marling, "America's Love Affair with the Automobile in the Television Age," in Wollen and Kerr, *Autopia*, 354.
6. Ibid., 358.
7. Jackle, Sculle, and Rodgers, *The Motel in America*, 18. See also *Management Manual for Motor Hotels*, ed. Alice L. Patterson (Chicago: Patterson, 1962).
8. Ackermann, *Cool Comfort*, 5.

Architectural Elements

1. Jackson, *'Contemporary,'* 23.
2. Lejeune and Shulman, *The Making of Miami Beach, 1933–1942*, 27.

Materials

1. Jackson, *'Contemporary,'* 205.
2. Nash and Robinson, *MiMo*, 69.
3. Jackson, *'Contemporary,'* 27.
4. Craig Vogel, "Aluminum: A Competitive Material of Choice in the Design of New Products, 1950 to the Present," in *Aluminum by Design*, 142.
5. Hine, *Populuxe*, 81.

Shapes

1. Hine, *Populuxe*, 88.
2. See Jackson, *'Contemporary,'* 147.
3. Hine, *Populuxe*, 114–17.

Shapiro Residence

1. Marcus, *Design in the Fifties*, 57.

Copa City Night Club

1. The text of the broadcast was reprinted in a local newspaper. See "Heatter Hails New Copa City as 'The Impossible Dream Come True,'" *Miami Beach Florida Sun*, December 28, 1948.

Motel Row

1. "5,000 Units Built along North Beach," *Miami Herald*, October 28, 1951; Martin, "Big Rush to the Sun," 71; "Motel Row Thrives on New Trend," *Miami Herald*, December 24, 1950.

Ocean Palm Motel

1. I learned many years later that a few two-story motels had actually been built before the Ocean Palm, though guest rooms were not available on both floors. Most documented two-story motels built before 1949 feature garages on the ground level; others include a single, second-story apartment for the motel manager or are built into a sloping site. Thus, the Ocean Palm can be considered the first motel to incorporate two levels of rentable guest rooms. See Mary Ann Beecher, "The Motel in Builder's Literature and Architectural Publications," in Jennings, *Roadside America*, 123; Witzel, *The American Motel*, 136; and Lightfoot et al., *Tourist Court Plan Book*, 15, 80, 1-A, 50-A.

2. As late as 1955, motel-industry publications acknowledged that "the elongated single-story plan [had] become associated in the public mind with motels." Convenience was the cornerstone of motel design, and a single-story building was believed to be more convenient than one with multiple levels. The experience of Albuquerque trader Charles Garrett Wallace was typical: "I was selling my Indian goods around the country and [at] every hotel I stopped at, I had to haul my rugs and jewelry up and down the stairs. I saw the need for motels. Didn't have to walk up and down those stairs. Park right at your door. It was a miracle." Baker and Funaro, *Motels*, 7; Jackle, Sculle, and Rodgers, *Motel in America*, 296.

3. "More Motel Than Hotel Rooms," 18; "Motels—and Women—Sometimes Need 'Face-lifting,'" 6; Baker and Funaro, *Motels*, 155. See also Nash and Robinson, *MiMo*, 90.

4. After World War II, variations of the resort motel also began popping up in vacation areas like Las Vegas, Nevada; Scottsdale, Arizona; Treasure Island, Florida; and Wildwood, New Jersey. The proliferation of the building type is discussed further in the next section.

The Resort Motel

1. Hine, *Populuxe*, 17.

2. Stedman and Stedman, "Miami's Miracle Mile of Motels," 10; "Motel Row," *Practical Builder* (1956): 30.

3. Baker and Funaro, *Motels*, 6.

Driftwood Motel

1. For an in-depth discussion of themed motels and hotels see Hess, *Viva Las Vegas*.

Thunderbird Motel

1. "More Motel Than Hotel Rooms," 18; Giller, "Design, Interiors and Construction," 3.

Suburban Housing

1. Baritz, *The Good Life*, 198.

Military Housing

1. Daniel H. Else, "Military Housing Privatization Initiative: Background and Issues," Library of Congress Congressional Research Service, July 2, 2001. Also available at <www.acq.osd.mil/housing/docs/crs.pdf>.
2. For an in-depth discussion of the U.S. Air Force's use of architecture in the mid-1950s to reinforce its modern image, see Bruegmann, *Modernism at Mid-Century*.

Supermarkets and Shopping Centers

1. The first store to identify itself as a supermarket was King Kullen in New York in 1930. Before 1950, supermarkets accounted for 35 percent of retail food sales; by 1960, this number had risen to 70 percent. Humphrey, *Shelf Life*, 69.
2. Ibid., 71. See also Hine, *Populuxe*, 24–25.
3. Liebs, *Main Street to Miracle Mile*, 129.
4. Ibid., 30.

Singapore Hotel

1. Miami's midcentury hotel architects adapted the superstructure and pedestal configuration from large Modernist office buildings like the Lever House (Skidmore, Owings, and Merrill, New York City, 1951). For more information, see Nash and Robinson, *MiMo*, 48, 53–85.

Diplomat Hotel and Country Club

1. The hotel's management wanted the building to be glamorous, not gaudy: "With some of Florida's flashier hotels having been tried and adjudged 'gilty' by the vacationing visitor, a different and tasteful approach will be offered by the new $23,000,000 Diplomat Hotel and Country Club." Diplomat Hotel and Country Club guest book, mid-December 1958, 16-A, in the author's possession.

Alliance for Progress

1. While the education, health, and infrastructure initiatives of the Alliance for Progress raised the standard of living in Latin America, the program was not as successful at furthering political stability in the region. For an in-depth analysis, see Scheman, *The Alliance for Progress*.

Florida Atlantic University

1. For an expanded discussion of the influence self-contained, monumental architecture had on interior and industrial design of the 1960s trends, see Jackson, *The Sixties*, 104–12.
2. Kahn, "Monumentality," 18.
3. FAU's Boca Raton campus has grown significantly since 1965. The construction of additional facilities has obscured the original single-axis campus plan.

Bibliography

Ackermann, Marsha E. *Cool Comfort: America's Romance with Air-Conditioning*. Washington, D.C.: Smithsonian Institution Press, 2002.

Adamson, Paul, and Marty Arbunich. *Eichler: Modernism Rebuilds the American Dream*. Salt Lake City: Gibbs Smith, 2002.

"Alliance for Progress Is on the Move in Panama." *Congressional Record* (September 27, 1962): A7162.

Aluminum by Design. Edited by Sarah Nichols. Pittsburgh: Carnegie Museum of Art, in association with Harry N. Abrams, 2000. An exhibition catalogue.

Baker, Geoffrey, and Bruno Funaro. *Motels*. New York: Reinhold, 1955.

Baritz, Loren. *The Good Life: The Meaning of Success for the American Middle Class*. New York: Knopf, 1989.

Bel Geddes, Norman. *Horizons*. Boston: Little, Brown, 1932.

Beyond the Box: Mid-Century Modern Architecture in Miami and New York. Edited by Teri D'Amico, and David Framberger. Miami Beach: Urban Arts Committee and the Municipal Art Society of New York, 2002. An exhibition catalogue.

Bruegmann, Robert, ed. *Modernism at Mid-Century: The Architecture of the United State Air Force Academy*. Chicago: University of Chicago Press, 1994.

"Carillon Is Tops on the Gold Coast." *Miami Herald*, August 11, 1957.

"Diplomat's the New Gold Coast Jewel." *Miami Herald*, December 14, 1958.

Giller, Norman M. *An Adventure in Architecture*. Miami Beach: Virgo Press, 1976.

———. "Architecturally Speaking." *Florida Building Journal* (January 1958).

———. *A Century in America*. Miami Beach: Virgo Press, 1986.

———. "Design, Interiors and Construction." In *Management Manual for Motor Hotels*, edited by Alice L. Patterson, 1–12. Chicago: Patterson, 1962.

———. "Motels Demand Planning." *Practical Builder* (1956): 23–28.

———. "Nighttime Architecture." *Florida Motel Journal*, 15, no.2 (March 1965): 4.

———. "The Role of the Architect-Banker." *Florida Contractor and Builder* (November 1971).

———. "Some Unmistakable Motel Trends as an Architect Sees Them." *American Motel Magazine* (March 1958).

"Giller Designs Unusual Small Home." *Miami Herald*, June 12, 1958.

Going, Going, Gone?: Mid-Century Architecture in South Florida. Edited by John O'Conner and Diane Smart. Ft. Lauderdale: Museum of Art Ft. Lauderdale, 2005. An exhibition catalogue.

Greenberg, Milton. *The G.I. Bill: The Law That Changed America*. New York: Lickle, 1997.

Hess, Alan. *Googie Redux: Ultramodern Roadside Architecture*. San Francisco: Chronicle Books, 2004.

———. *Viva Las Vegas: After-Hours Architecture*. San Francisco: Chronicle Books, 1993.

Hess, Alan, and Andrew Danish. *Palm Springs Weekend: The Architecture and Design of a Midcentury Oasis*. San Francisco: Chronicle Books, 2001.

Hine, Thomas. *Populuxe: From Tailfins and TV Dinners to Barbie Dolls and Fallout Shelters*. New York: MJF Books, 1986.

Hochstim, Jan. *Florida Modern: Residential Architecture 1945–1970*. New York: Rizzoli, 2004.

Holland, Harry. *Travellers' Architecture*. London: George G. Harrap, 1971.

Humphrey, Kim. *Shelf Life: Supermarkets and the Changing Cultures of Consumption*. Cambridge: Cambridge University Press, 1998.

Jackle, John A., Keith A. Sculle, and Jefferson S. Rodgers. *The Motel in America*. Baltimore: Johns Hopkins University Press, 1996.

Jackson, Lesley. *'Contemporary': Architecture and Interiors of the 1950s*. London: Phaidon, 1994.

———. *The Sixties: Decade of Design Revolution*. London: Phaidon, 1998.

Jennings, Jan, ed. *Roadside America: The Automobile in Design and Culture*. Ames: Iowa State University Press, 1990.

Juntunen, Arthur. "'Motel Row' Lures Vacationers." *Detroit Free Press Roto Magazine*, March 14, 1954: 6–7.

Kahn, Louis I. "Monumentality." In *Louis I. Kahn: Writings, Lectures, Interviews*, edited by Alessandra Latour. New York: Rizzoli, 1991: 18–27.

Kennedy, John F. "Preliminary Formulations of the Alliance for Progress." Address at a White House reception for Latin American diplomats and members of Congress, Washington, D.C., March 13, 1961. *Department of State Bulletin* 44, no. 1136 (April 3, 1961): 471–74.

Lapidus, Morris. *Too Much Is Never Enough: An Autobiography*. New York: Rizzoli, 1996.

Le Corbusier. *Towards a New Architecture*. London: John Rodker, 1931. Translation of the 13th French edition with a new introduction by Frederick Etchells. Reprint, New York: Dover, 1986. Page references are to the 1986 edition.

Lejeune, Jean-Francois, and Allan T. Shulman. *The Making of Miami Beach, 1933–1942: The Architecture of Lawrence Murray Dixon*. New York: Rizzoli, 2000.

Lewin, Susan Grant, ed. *Formica & Design: From the Countertop to High Art*. New York: Rizzoli, 1991.

Liebs, Chester H. *Main Street to Miracle Mile: American Roadside Architecture*. Boston: Little, Brown, 1985.

Lightfoot, Tom E., Bob Gresham, Hill Gresham, and Jewell A. Berry. *Tourist Court Plan Book*. 2nd ed. Temple, Tex.: Tourist Court Journal, 1950.

Marcus, George H. *Design in the Fifties: When Everyone Went Modern*. Munich/New York: Prestel, 1998.

Marling, Karal Ann. *As Seen on TV: The Visual Culture of Everyday Life in the 1950s*. Cambridge, Mass.: Harvard University Press, 1994.

Martin, Ralph G. "Big Rush to the Sun: Taking an Amazing 250-Mile Journey in Florida." *Newsweek*, January 17, 1955: 67–75.

"More Motel Than Hotel Rooms Next Five Years Predicted by Prominent Miami Beach Architect." *Room & Food Service Magazine* 7, no. 8 (1959): 18.

"Motels—and Women—Sometimes Need 'Face-lifting.'" *Florida Motel Journal* 11, no. 10 (1961): 6–7.

Nash, Eric P., and Randall C. Robinson Jr. *MiMo: Miami Modernism Revealed*. San Francisco: Chronicle Books, 2004.

Rielly, Edward J. *The 1960s*. Westport, Conn.: Greenwood Press, 2003.

Sasser, Michael W. "At 83, Architect Has Left His MiMo Mark on the City." *Miami Herald*, November 18, 2001.

Scheman, L. Ronald, ed. *The Alliance for Progress: A Retrospective*. New York: Praeger, 1988.

Schudel, Matt. "Meet the Man Who Made Miami Modern." *South Florida Sun-Sentinel*, November 4, 2001.

Stedman, Gerald, and Margaret Stedman. "Miami's Miracle Mile of Motels." *Tourist Court Journal* (July 1952).

"Thunderbird to be Tourist Dream." *Miami Beach Sun*, August 21, 1955.

Trelles, Emma. "Modern Love." *The Street*, November 2–8, 2001.

Venturi, Robert, Denise Scott Brown, and Steven Izenour. *Learning from Las Vegas*. Cambridge, Mass.: MIT Press, 1972.

Werne, Jo. "'Demand Good Design,' Architect Tells Public." *Miami Herald*, April 17, 1977.

Witzel, Michael. *The American Motel*. Osceola, Wash.: MBI, 2000.

Wollen, Peter, and Joe Kerr, eds. *Autopia: Cars and Culture*. London: Reaktion, 2002.

Photo Credits

Ardmore Studio

Art Apple/Associated Photographers

Black/Baker Photographers

Joseph B. Brignolo

Peter R. Bromer

Paul L. Date

Thomas Delbeck for North Beach Development Corporation and Urban Arts Committee of Miami Beach, from the exhibition titled *Beyond the Box: Mid-Century Modern Architecture in Miami and New York*.

Courtesy *Detroit Free Press*

Klara Farkas

Ray Fisher

Andrew Friedman

Walter Gray

Courtesy *Harper's Bazaar*

Robin Hill

Hinman Photography

Historical Museum of Southern Florida

The Miami Herald

John H. McGonigal

Postcard collection of Larry Wiggins

Pilkington North America, Inc.

RADA Photography

State Archives of Florida

Gene Troop

Courtesy U.S. Air Force

Kurt Waldman

Larry Ward

Warner-Murray Studio

All other images courtesy Giller & Giller, Inc., Archives.

Index

Cuban Missile Crisis, *133*
Curves, 29–30

D'Amico, Teri, 2
Department of Defense, 75, 83
Design Review Board, 147
Diplomat Country Club, *xii,* 1, 123, 148, 152n1; beginnings of, 114; Calcutta Room in, *114, 115;* clubhouse of, *114;* golf course of, 114–15, *123;* water shuttle transportation to, 116
Diplomat Hotel, *xii,* 1, *117,* 123, 125, 148; aerial view of, *123;* circles used in, 122, *122;* decorating scheme of, *119,* 120; design of, 118; grand lobby of, *119–20;* landscaping of, *113;* lounges in, *121;* luxurious accommodations of, *121;* management of, 152n1; rendering of, *118*
Diplomatic architecture, 131
Dixon, L. Murray, 1
Driftwood Motel, 59, *59–61,* 148; design of, 62; owners of, 61, 65; postcard of, *62;* TV room in, *63*

Eastern Airlines Cafeteria, *142, 143,* 144, *145,* 149; time-study analysis, *143;* traffic-flow chart, *144*
Eden Roc Hotel, 23
Eichler, Joseph, 18
Elementary Schools, *128,* 149

Elevators, 65, 97
Envoy Motel, 114, *115–16;* aluminum tables/ chairs in, *26;* design of, 115–16; ground-floor plan of, *117;* location of, 118. *See also* Diplomat Country Club; Diplomat Hotel
Executive Motor Hotel, 100, 103, 105, 149; advertisement featuring, *105;* dining room, *103;* ground-floor plan, *104;* lobby of, *102;* postcard of, *100*

Fallingwater, 15
Federal Housing Administration (FHA), 71
Fein, Gilbert M., vi
FHA. *See* Federal Housing Administration
"Five Points Towards a New Architecture" (Le Corbusier), 17
Flat roofs, 17–18, 39, *40;* on "House with Four Faces," *70;* in military housing, 78
Flat-slab construction, 107–8
Floor plans: Envoy Motel, *117;* Executive Motor Hotel, *104;* Giller Building, *91;* Key West Naval Air Station, *77;* Shapiro Residence, *43*
Florida. *See* South Florida
Florida Atlantic University, 135–37, 149, 152n3; Classroom Building, *136,* 137; College of Business Administration, *134,* 135–37, *136;* College of Education, *134,* 135–37, *136*

Florida hotels: Carillon Hotel, 25, 28, *106–11, 107–10,* 148; Diplomat Hotel, *xii,* 1, *113, 117–23, 118,* 120–23, 125, 148, 152n1; Eden Roc Hotel, 23; Shelbourne Hotel, *8,* 10; Singapore Hotel, *96–99, 97, 99,* 149
Florida motels: Carib Motel, 56–57, *56–58,* 59; Chateau Motel, *31;* design of, 9; Driftwood Motel, 59, *59–63,* 61–62, 65, 148; Envoy Motel, *26,* 114–18, *115–17;* Ocean Palm Motel, *vii, 51–54, 52–53,* 56, 61, 105, 148, 151n1; resort, *54, 55,* 151n4; Thunderbird Motel, *64–67,* 65, 67, 97, 113, 148. *See also* Motel Row
Florida Room, 42, 44
Fluid forms, 31
Fontainebleau Hotel, 113
Food Fair: shopping centers, *86, 87,* 148; supermarkets, *84,* 85–86, 148
Formica, 26–27; boomerang shapes on, 31; in InterAmerican Bank, 140; pattern varieties of, *27*
France, Roy F., 2
F&R Builders, 72–73
Friedland, Sam, 85, 113, 114, 115, 123
Futurama, 7–8, 61

General Electric Corporation, 81
Giller, Charles, *38*

Cafeteria, 144; in Food Fair Shopping Centers, 87; in Thunderbird Motel, 67
Polevitzky, Igor B., vi, *8*, 10
Pollack, Paul, 61, 62, 65
Pool, kidney-shaped, 31, *31*
Praver, William, 97
Pulmanette kitchens, 56
PVC piping, 82–83

Ransome, Ernest, 21
Renderings: Carillon Hotel, *106*; Copa City Nightclub, *46*; Diplomat Hotel, *118*; Eastern Airlines Cafeteria, *145*; Homestead Air Force Base, *74, 78–79*; Key West Naval Air Station, *76*; of Morey Giller Apartments, *38*; North Shore Community Center, *126*; of suburban housing, *69*
Residence: Giller, *17–18*, 148; Shapiro, 42–44, *42–44*
Residential communities: Coral Way Village, 72–73, *72–73*; designs of, 130; examples of houses in, *69–71*; military housing, *74*, 75–83, *76, 78–79*; postwar demand for, 69; Sebring Hills Housing Development, *13, 68*, 148. *See also* Military housing; Suburban housing
Resort motel, *54*, 55, 151n4. *See also* Motel Row

Robinson, Randall, viii, 1
Roman brick, 23, 62. *See also* Brick
Roosevelt, Franklin D., 69
Rosen, Arnold, 72
Rubel, Melvin G., 97
Rubiyat Hotel, 97, *98*, 139, 148

SAC, 80
Sahara Motel, *101*
Sebring Hills Housing Development, *13, 68*, 148
Seman, Emmanuel, 52–53
Shapes: boomerang, 31; kidney, 31, *31*; streamlined, *7*, 30, 78
Shapiro, Herbert, 43
Shapiro Residence, *44*; first-floor plan of, *43*; model of, *42*, 42–44
Shelbourne Hotel, *8*, 10
Singapore Hotel, *96*, 97, 149; original concept for, *98*; promotional brochure for, *99*; success of, 99
Skyscrapers, 8, 25
Smit, Jan, 5, 135
Solomon R. Guggenheim Museum, 30, 97
South Florida: abundance of limestone in, 21; architects, 9; climate of, 18; development of, 147; parking garages in, 10; postwar building

boom in, *35*; resort motels, 53; tourism industry, 69; visual interest in structures of, 23
Speyer, Sven, 5
Staircases, 15, 39; in Executive Motor Hotel, *103*; in Giller Building, 93; gold anodized aluminum, 121; hanging, 120
Stern, Henry, 100, *101*
Stone, 23
Stone, Edward Durell, vii
Strategic Air Command (SAC), 80
Streamline Moderne, 29
Streamlining, 30, 78
Suburban housing: designs, 130; exterior view of, *70*; "House with Four Faces" as, 71, *71*. *See also* Residential communities
Sullivan, Louis, 3, 39
Sunny Isles: bridge in honor of Giller, 147; Carib Motel in, 56–57, *56–58*, 59; Chateau Motel in, *31*; commissions, 148–49; Driftwood Motel in, 59, *59–63*, 61–62, 65, 148; economic development of, 140; InterAmerican National Bank in, *138, 140*; Motel Row in, *50*, 113; need for bank in, 139; Ocean Palm Motel, *vii, 51–54*, 52–53, 56, 61, 105, 148, 151n1; Thunderbird Motel, *64–67*, 65, 67, 97, 113, 148. *See also* Motel Row

Supermarket, 85, 152n1; space for cars provided at, 86. *See also* Food Fair

Teague, Walter Dorwin, 45
Television, 62, *63*
Thunderbird Motel, 65, 67, 97, 113, 148; advertisement for, *65*; brochure for, *67*; lobby of, *66*; postcard of, *64*
Treister, Kenneth, vi
Tubular aluminum folding chairs, 26
Two-story motels, 52, 151n1

U.S. AID (Agency for the International Development of the U.S. State Department), 129–33

van der Rohe, Mies, 15, 24, 25, 103, 135, 139
Venturi, Robert, 103, 150n2

Walters, Barbara, 110
Walters, Lou, 110
Weatherton heat pump, 81, 83
Weinger, Murray, 45, 47, *48*

Windows, 12; asymmetrically placed, 145; of Carillon Hotel, *107*; display, 87; of Giller Building, 93; glass jalousie, 24
Woolworth's, 87, *87*
World War II, 2, *136*, 151n4; air-conditioning developed following, 11; challenge of building after, 69; conclusion of, 3; demand for aluminum during, 25; economic boom after, *55*; military housing shortage following, 75; onset of, 8
Wright, Frank Lloyd, 15, 30; elements introduced by, viii; Prairie-style house designs, 19

Norman M. Giller, FAIA, received a bachelor of architecture degree from the University of Florida in 1945. After founding norman m. giller & associates in 1946, Giller went on to design over ten thousand structures in Florida and elsewhere. Giller is the author of *An Adventure in Architecture* (1976) and *A Century in America* (1986). He is a longtime resident of Miami Beach.

Sarah Giller Nelson, a Miami-born art and architectural historian, has spent her entire life admiring her grandfather's architecture. She received a B.A. in the history of art and architecture from Brown University and an M.A. in modern art history, theory, and criticism from the School of the Art Institute of Chicago. She currently lives in Chicago.

Books of related interest from University Press of Florida

The Architecture of Leisure:
The Florida Resort Hotels of
Henry Flagler and Henry Plant
Susan R. Braden

The Architecture of James Gamble
Rogers II in Winter Park, Florida
Patrick W. McClane and
Debra A. McClane

Coral Gables: Miami Riviera:
An Architectural Guide
Aristides J. Millas and
Ellen J. Uguccioni

Florida's Colonial
Architectural Heritage
Elsbeth K. Gordon

Jacksonville's Architectural
Heritage: Landmarks for the Future
Wayne W. Wood

The Houses of St. Augustine,
1565–1821
Albert Manucy

Pioneer of Tropical Landscape
Architecture: William Lyman
Phillips in Florida
Faith Reyher Jackson

Saving South Beach
M. Barron Stofik

The Southern Movie Palace:
Rise, Fall, and Resurrection
Janna Jones

For more information on these
and other books, visit our Web
site at www.upf.com.